Attaining the 2030 Sustainable Development Goal of Life on Land

FAMILY BUSINESSES ON A MISSION

Griffith UNIVERSITY
Queensland, Australia

Series Editor:

Naomi Birdthistle

The Family Businesses on a Mission series examines how the United Nations Sustainable Development Goals (UN SDGs) can be applied in family businesses around the world, providing insights into cultural and societal differences and displaying innovative approaches to complex environmental and societal issues.

Other Titles in This Series

Attaining the 2030 Sustainable Development Goal of Life on Land

EDITED BY

NAOMI BIRDTHISTLE
Griffith University, Australia

emerald
PUBLISHING

United Kingdom – North America – Japan – India – Malaysia – China

Emerald Publishing Limited
Emerald Publishing, Floor 5, Northspring, 21-23 Wellington Street, Leeds LS1 4DL

First edition 2025

Reprints and permissions service
Contact: www.copyright.com

British Library Cataloguing in Publication Data
A catalogue record for this book is available from the British Library

ISBN: 978-1-83608-215-6 (Print)
ISBN: 978-1-83608-212-5 (Online)
ISBN: 978-1-83608-214-9 (Epub)

INVESTOR IN PEOPLE

Contents

List of Figures and Tables

Figures

Tables

About the Editor

Professor Naomi Birdthistle has entrepreneurship and family business running through her veins. She tried to work in her family business when she was four but was told she was too small. She came back year after year asking to work, and eventually, her grandmother capitulated and let her work in the family business when she was seven. After years of working in the family business part-time and having completed her studies at Stirling University, Babson College, Harvard University and the University of Limerick, Naomi established her own consulting business, consulting family businesses in her hometown. She is now a Professor of Entrepreneurship and Business Innovation at Griffith University, teaching future family business leaders and researching family business issues as well. Naomi is an award-winning academic having received numerous awards for her teaching and her research.

About the Contributors

Professor Mary Barrett, Faculty of Business and Law, University of Wollongong, Australia. Mary Barrett is an Honorary Professor of Management in the Faculty of Business and Law at the University of Wollongong, Australia. Her research interests include entrepreneurship, leadership, business communication and gender in management, especially how these play out in family firms and different national contexts. Though formally retired, Mary continues to research, supervise higher-degree students and review articles for academic publications. Her publications include seven books and numerous research articles in refereed journals. Mary's most recent book, *Women in Family Business: New Perspectives, Contexts and Roles* (Edward Elgar, 2024) was co-edited with Dr Jolien Huybrechts and Professor Jean Lee. With Emeritus Professor Ken Moores AM, Mary has also written two other chapters in this series on the UN Sustainable Development Goals (SDGs): one on Outland Denim, for the chapter on Decent Work and Economic Growth (SDG#8), and another on Wagner Corporation and its Airport for Industry, Innovation and Infrastructure (SDG#9).

Dr Allan Discua Cruz is the Director of the Centre for Family Business and member of the Pentland Centre for Sustainability in Business and at Lancaster University Management School (United Kingdom). His current research interests relate to entrepreneurship by families in business. He has published in journals such as *Entrepreneurship and Regional Development*, *Journal of Business Research*, *Journal of Business Ethics*, *Entrepreneurship Theory and Practice*, *International Journal of Entrepreneurial Behaviour and Research*, *Journal of Family Business Management* and *International Small Business Journal* among others. He is currently co-editing a special issue on entrepreneurship and poverty in the *Entrepreneurship and Regional Development Journal*. He has published three cases in this series related to SDG#1, SDG#8, SDG#11 and SDG#13.

Gina Dang is a visionary leader transforming Australian agriculture with innovation and excellence. As General Manager of SSS Strawberries, she inspires her team with passion and expertise. Gina's journey began in 1994 when her family emigrated from Vietnam to Australia. She and her six siblings co-founded SSS Strawberries (Seven Successful Siblings), now one of Australia's largest and most innovative strawberry farms, renowned for its excellence and sustainability. Her love for food led her to launch Gina's Table, offering frozen and freeze-dried fruit products from Australia's largest state-of-the-art facility. Gina is a multi-talented entrepreneur, balancing roles as a Human Resources

Trainer, a Manager, an Advisor, a CEO and a Director of her family business. Gina oversees the business's property development and management arm, using her Principal real estate licence and her bachelor's degree in Commercial Law and Accounting. She is a Master of NLP and is an Australian Institute of Company Directors graduate.

Dr Jacinta Dsilva is a Research Director at SEE Institute, a hub for sustainability research, education and innovation in Dubai, United Arab Emirates. In her current role, she spearheads the research department and focuses on areas such as sustainability, behavioural studies and circular economy in the built environment sector. She completed her PhD from Coventry University, UK, and holds two master's degrees in Consumer Behaviour and Human Resources Management. She is the author of several books such as 'Business Communication' and 'Surviving the COVID-19 Pandemic' and 'SDG-5: Gender Equality & Female Empowerment Policy for Sustainable Development'. She has several research publications under her belt both in marketing and sustainability. Another area of interest is researching family-run businesses that have developed a sustainable model of operations that has positively impacted the society at large. These research studies highlight how businesses successfully balance growth and social responsibility, serving as models for sustainable entrepreneurship.

Rosemary L. Fisher applies entrepreneurship principles to create a culture of creativity and adaptability in contemporary learning environments using evidence-based teaching strategies, with a passion for fostering innovation and problem-solving. Her research expertise informs her teaching practice, allowing her to design personalised approaches that enhance student engagement, motivation and learning outcomes. In addition to her commitment to education, Rosemary has a strong interest in sustainable practices. By combining her expertise in research with her concern for the environment, Rosemary seeks out unique insights and perspectives that contribute to the broader discussion on sustainable entrepreneurship and education for a more sustainable future.

Associate Professor Rob Hales is the discipline leader for Sustainable Business and Management in the Department of Business Strategy and Innovation. His research interests focus on the governance issues around the grand challenges of our time. Furthermore, his research focuses on SDGs in business and government, a business case for climate change, climate change policy, carbon management, sustainable tourism and working with First Peoples on consent processes and climate change. He was the first programme director of Griffith University's Master of Global Development. He teaches in the Department of Business Strategy and Innovation and has convened master's level courses such as Leadership for Sustainable Business, Research Methods for Policy Makers and Sustainability and Systems Thinking. He supervises PhD students in the areas of collaborative governance, sustainability transitions and climate change.

Dr Amber Marshall is a Lecturer in Management at Griffith University (Australia) whose research focuses on digital inclusion and rural development. Her work explores how individuals, organisations and communities in regional, rural and remote Australia become digitally connected and adopt digital technologies, and how this intersects with social and economic well-being. Dr Marshall's work draws on interdisciplinary perspectives from management and communication sciences and employs qualitative and ethnographic methods to co-design solutions with local stakeholders. Her research interests include digital AgTech and data, digital inclusion ecosystems, remote telecommunications infrastructure and digital skills and capability development. She has published in top-tiered journals, presented at national and international conferences, produced industry and policy reports and attracted substantial research funding from government and commercial partners.

Claudio G. Muller is a Visiting Professor of Management at Rawls College of Business, Texas Tech University, United States. Dr Muller has published in journals in the field of management such as: *Journal of Family Business Strategy*, *Journal of Evolutionary Studies in Business*, *Cross Cultural & Strategic Management*, *Academia Revista Latinoamericana de Gestión*, *British Food Journal* and *Global Journal of Flexible Systems Management* among others. He is also the co-author of the books *Family Firms in Latin America* (edited by Routledge, 2018) and *Family Business Heterogeneity in Latin America* (edited by Springer, 2021).

Marcio Paz is the cofounder and the Director of Operations of Del Lago Orgánico S de RL. He is a Chemical Engineering graduate with postgraduate degrees in Project Management and Strategic Planning. He is currently mentoring his children in all the business areas in Del Lago Orgánico S de RL.

Rebeca Paz is the cofounder of the family business Del Lago Orgánico S de RL. She is a Marketing and Logistics Engineering graduate. Currently, she is the legal representative and general manager of Del Lago Orgánico S de RL.

Michael J. A. Seidler, an engineer with the soul of an environmentalist, holds a Bachelor of Engineering (Elec.) and an MBA from the University of Melbourne. He commenced his professional career in the construction industry as a building services engineer, developing lighting and power solutions for commercial and industrial developments. With time, he expanded his expertise into building automation, industrial process automation and data networking. Transitioning into the mobile telecommunications industry, he spent more than 20 years in technology strategy, product management and development and business analysis and strategy. More recently, he has been working with a focus on renewable energy and environmentally conscious housing solutions and the contribution they can make to greenhouse gas reduction.

Marina Skinner, founder and principal of Generational Harmony, is a leading Australian family business specialist with over 20 years of experience. She holds an EMBA in Family Business from Bond University and has 12 years of hands-on experience managing a small family business, earning a Business Achiever of the Year Award. As a Specialist Accredited Family Business Advisor (SAFBA), she has worked with major international firms like BDO and Grant Thornton, where she helped create the award-winning Family Office Services division. Marina co-authored the 'Family Business Wealth & Knowledge Transfer Report', which influenced the appointment of the Australian Small Business and Family Enterprise Ombudsman. She is a strategic mentor who ensures best practices and generational continuity for her clients through a holistic business approach. Marina is affiliated with the Family Business Association (FBA) and a judge in the FBA Awards for Family Business Excellence.

Mrs Nikki Thompson has always been a generalist and a visionary who has always followed her heart. She met and fell in love with Peter as a young physiotherapy student and brought those skills with her when she moved to Echo Hills 43 years ago. She has always loved to mix evidence-based practice with more ancient wisdom during her career as a health professional, her coaching career and in her connection with the life on the land at Echo Hills. Her journey with the land has been a gift, and while not 'working in the paddock' much, her passion for what comes when we all work on 'the inner paddock between our ears' has added different dimension to the emergence of their family and life at Echo Hills.

Mr Peter Thompson was born and raised at Echo Hills walking its land his whole life. He is a farmer who is passionate about agriculture with an emphasis on regenerative practices and its valuable contribution to modern society. He believes in operating as a team in conjunction with his urban counterparts for the long-term financial and environmental sustainability of Australia. He has a life-long love of machinery and technology, especially where it can enhance the human experience. He is a curious innovator who reads and travels widely. He likes to find the techniques that can be trialed and tested in local context rather than devoutly following a particular practice. Peter is totally committed to seeing a fair and equitable integration of energy and agricultural production that first and foremost protects the land, water, agricultural practices and human live-ability for future generations.

Foreword

Prof. Walter Leal Filho (PhD, DSc, DPhil, DTech, DEd)
Chair, Inter-University Sustainable Development Research Programme

The SDGs adopted by the United Nations General Assembly in September 2015 provide a universal call to action to end poverty, protect the planet and ensure that by 2030 all people enjoy peace and prosperity.

They also entail elements of importance towards a strategic business engagement with sustainability issues. These offer a framework which provides businesses with a systematic approach to identify new business opportunities while contributing to the solution of the grand sustainability challenges facing the world today, including climate change. Each SDG, if achieved, will have a direct and significant positive impact on millions of people's lives around the world and the environment in which they live. Businesses have an opportunity to widen the purpose of business through adopting the SDGs as targets for their operations. Thus, they can make a meaningful contribution to the greater good through achieving their operational objectives.

Family businesses are uniquely placed to contribute to SDGs for many reasons. Firstly, because family business models have longer time perspectives, and this allows the family business to link with the longer-term SDG time frame – 2030. Second, family businesses often focus on aspects of business operation which do not have an immediate return on investment such as relationship building with stakeholder groups. Thirdly, family businesses tend to rate the importance of ethics higher than standard businesses and thus align well with the social dimensions of the SDGs. Lastly, family businesses have intergenerational perspectives which is a core principle of sustainability.

This book provides insights into how family business operationalises SDG#15: Life on Land. The book uses a rigorous case study approach for family businesses to detail aspects of their business which help life on land. The cases provided here are living proofs that family business that operates for the greater good actually works! Non-family businesses can take a leaf out of the family businesses portrayed in this book as they can provide different perspectives on how businesses can successfully align SDGs and business strategy.

Despite many businesses having adopted environmental social governance strategies and environmental management systems, the effect of this activity has not been reflected in a healthier planet. Many 'state of the environment' reports indicate that planetary health is decreasing, and planetary boundaries are being crossed or are about to be crossed. While the cause of this decline is not entirely the fault of business, there still needs to be a greater effort to address the decline. The challenge for family businesses is to use their unique characteristics and set ambitious programmes of work that make a meaningful contribution to achieving global goals. This book provides insights into how family businesses can achieve such a mission and how non-family businesses can be inspired to do the same.

Acknowledgements

The Editor would like to thank the contributors of the book for providing insights and sharing learnings from their business practice. We acknowledge that writing up cases in the format required considerable time and effort. The quality of the cases presented is testament to their efforts.

The Editor would also like to thank Emerald Publishing for supporting the publication of this book and the mission for deeper sustainability through utilising the SDGs.

Dr Amber Marshall, Mrs Nikki Thompson and Mr Peter Thompson, authors of Chapter 4, acknowledge the traditional owners of the land where Echo Hills Farm is situated, on Yiman country in Queensland. We give gratitude to all those who have walked, lived and cared for this land since humans evolved in this place. We have been and always will be owned and grown by this land. May we all remember that as we journey forward together collaboratively as true custodians.

Gina Dang, the co-author of Chapter 6, wishes to take this opportunity to express her heartfelt gratitude to her entire family: her husband Toan Nguyen, her siblings, Victor, Lilly, Cindy, Thanh, Trinity and Rena Dang for their relevant contributions, expertise, insightful discussions and suggestions which greatly improved the quality of this case. Finally, Gina Dang would like to thank her parents and spiritual mentors from Tao for their endless love and support, without which this family business story would not have been possible.

Prof Mary Barrett, the author of Chapter 7, would like to thank Charlie Emery, the Managing Director of SOILCO, for the interview he granted very early on a business day, and for his help with access to website resources. She would also like to thank his staff for making the interview arrangements. Thanks are also due to SOILCO's founders Maria Emery and Tony Emery, who generously gave her a tour of SOILCO in about 2011. Tony Emery surely sowed the seed for this chapter when he remarked to her, 'You think you've seen compost? I'll show you compost!'

Dr Jacinta Dsilva, the author of Chapter 8, would like to take this opportunity to express her heartfelt gratitude to Mr Alaa Mustafa for generously sharing his valuable time for the interview and giving her and her research assistant, Lydia Cherian, valuable information to complete this case study. My sincere acknowledgement goes to Lydia Cherian, my research Intern and Ivory the staff member of MyHive for their unwavering support in completing this case.

Chapter 1

The Sustainable Development Goals: SDG#15 Life on Land and Family Business

Rob Hales

Griffith University, Australia

Introduction

The 2030 Agenda for Sustainable Development, adopted by all United Nations member states in 2015, serves as a shared blueprint for promoting peace, prosperity and well-being worldwide. The Sustainable Development Goals (SDGs) call for innovative solutions to complex societal and environmental issues. Businesses, particularly family enterprises, play a vital role in advancing these goals, as they constitute a significant portion of the global economy. The 2030 Agenda urges all nations to address critical challenges such as poverty, inequality, climate change, environmental degradation, peace and justice. These challenges are identified by 17 SDGs as depicted in Fig. 1.1 and within the SDGs are a total of 169 targets.

The 17 SDGs acknowledge that ending poverty and other global challenges need strategies that improve health and education, reduce inequality and spur economic growth – all while tackling climate change and working to preserve our oceans and forests (United Nations, 2021). This book makes an important contribution to research on family businesses by highlighting how businesses can make valuable contributions towards sustainable development and in particular assist in achieving the SDGs.

The adoption of SDG#15 is aligned with other business sustainability initiatives. Corporate businesses are increasingly adopting initiatives such as the Science Based Targets for Nature (n.d.), the Taskforce on Nature-related Financial Disclosures (TCFD, n.d.) and Target 10 of the Global Biodiversity Framework (Convention on Biological Diversity, 2022). The challenge for family businesses is to follow these types of frameworks that align with SDG#15. Although there is a growing list of initiatives aimed at increasing the environmental and social governance of companies in relation to biodiversity management, a focus on SDG#15 and the targets is a simple but deep approach to biodiversity preservation and management for a family business. When using the

Attaining the 2030 Sustainable Development Goal of Life on Land, 1–12
Copyright © 2025 Rob Hales
Published under exclusive licence by Emerald Publishing Limited
doi:10.1108/978-1-83608-212-520241001

Fig. 1.1.   17 Sustainable Development Goals.
Source: United Nations (2021).[1]

SDGs as a strategy to improve the elements within any goal, it is vital to use specific targets of each goal. These targets then need to be translated into business action.

Book Series Focus – SDG#15

This book focuses on SDG number 15 (SDG#15), which focuses on life on land. The main targets for SDG#15 are shown in Table 1.1. These targets can assist family businesses align business value chains with greater impact towards SDG#15 – to protect, restore and promote sustainable use of terrestrial ecosystems, sustainably manage forests, combat desertification and halt and reverse land degradation and halt biodiversity loss.

To help businesses understand and implement these targets and indicators, various authorities have produced guidance documents. Two commonly used guidance documents are the SDG guides from the Global Reporting Initiative (2019) and the United Nations Global Compact (n.d.). These documents provide a range of actions which businesses can implement to assist in achieving the targets. By aligning their strategies and operations with these targets, businesses can not only mitigate their environmental impact but also create long-term value

---

[1]The content of this publication has not been approved by the United Nations and does not reflect the views of the United Nations or its officials or Member States.

Table 1.1. SDG#15 Targets and Indicators.

SDG#15 Targets	SDG#15 Indicators
15.1 By 2020, ensure the conservation, restoration and sustainable use of terrestrial and inland freshwater ecosystems and their services, in particular forests, wetlands, mountains and drylands, in line with obligations under international agreements	15.1.1 Forest area as a proportion of total land area 15.1.2 Proportion of important sites for terrestrial and freshwater biodiversity that are covered by protected areas, by ecosystem type
15.2 By 2020, promote the implementation of sustainable management of all types of forests, halt deforestation, restore degraded forests and substantially increase afforestation and reforestation globally	15.2.1 Progress towards sustainable forest management
15.3 By 2030, combat desertification, restore degraded land and soil, including land affected by desertification, drought and floods, and strive to achieve a land degradation-neutral world	15.3.1 Proportion of land that is degraded over total land area
15.4 By 2030, ensure the conservation of mountain ecosystems, including their biodiversity, in order to enhance their capacity to provide benefits that are essential for sustainable development	15.4.1 Coverage by protected areas of important sites for mountain biodiversity 15.4.2 Mountain Green Cover Index
15.5 Take urgent and significant action to reduce the degradation of natural habitats, halt the loss of biodiversity and, by 2020, protect and prevent the extinction of threatened species	15.5.1 Red List Index
15.6 Promote fair and equitable sharing of the benefits arising from the utilisation of genetic resources and promote appropriate access to such resources, as internationally agreed	15.6.1 The number of countries that have adopted legislative, administrative and policy frameworks to ensure fair and equitable sharing of benefits

(Continued)

Table 1.1. *(Continued)*

SDG#15 Targets	SDG#15 Indicators
15.7 Take urgent action to end poaching and trafficking of protected species of flora and fauna and address both demand and supply of illegal wildlife products	15.7.1 Proportion of traded wildlife that was poached or illicitly trafficked
15.8 By 2020, introduce measures to prevent the introduction and significantly reduce the impact of invasive alien species on land and water ecosystems and control or eradicate the priority species	15.8.1 Proportion of countries adopting relevant national legislation and adequately resourcing the prevention or control of invasive alien species
15.9 By 2020, integrate ecosystem and biodiversity values into national and local planning, development processes, poverty reduction strategies and accounts	15.9.1 (a) The number of countries that have established national targets in accordance with or similar to Aichi Biodiversity Target 2 of the Strategic Plan for Biodiversity 2011–2020 in their national biodiversity strategy and action plans and the progress reported towards these targets and (b) integration of biodiversity into national accounting and reporting systems, defined as implementation of the System of Environmental-Economic Accounting
15.a Mobilise and significantly increase financial resources from all sources to conserve and sustainably use biodiversity and ecosystems	15.a.1 (a) Official development assistance on conservation and sustainable use of biodiversity and (b) revenue generated and finance mobilised from biodiversity-relevant economic instruments
15.b Mobilise significant resources from all sources and at all levels to finance sustainable forest management and provide adequate incentives to developing countries to advance such management, including for conservation and reforestation	15.b.1 (a) Official development assistance on conservation and sustainable use of biodiversity and 15.b.1 (b) revenue generated and finance mobilised from biodiversity-relevant economic instruments

Table 1.1. *(Continued)*

SDG#15 Targets	SDG#15 Indicators
15.c Enhance global support for efforts to combat poaching and trafficking of protected species, including by increasing the capacity of local communities to pursue sustainable livelihood opportunities	15.c.1 Proportion of traded wildlife that was poached or illicitly trafficked

Source: United Nations (n.d.).

for their stakeholders and the communities in which they operate. Some important ways that family business can align their business practices with SDG#15 and the challenges of alignment are provided below.

Target 15.1 – Preserving Terrestrial and Freshwater Ecosystems

Businesses that directly have operations in land and freshwater areas will have regulations relating to sustainable use, and this will vary in regulatory strength depending on where the business is located. The family businesses that have sustainability at the core will have adopted preservation and sustainability practices that go beyond minimal compliance standards. Family businesses situated in rural locations or near natural habitats also can contribute to the preservation and sustainable use of terrestrial and freshwater ecosystems. However, it depends on how sustainability is positioned concerning the business model of the organisation and how the business is linked to the local communities in which they are situated (Krause et al., 2020).

Target 15.2 – Sustainable Forest Management and Reforestation

For family businesses involved in forestry, agriculture or related sectors, adopting sustainable forest management practices is crucial. Businesses directly related to forestry must prioritise biodiversity preservation and sustainable management, guided by a range of forestry certification standards. One of the most prominent standards is the Programme for the Endorsement of Forest Certification (PEFC). This standard lays out international requirements that national forest management standards must meet for PEFC endorsement. For family businesses aiming to be sustainable, labelling schemes for certified forest products are vital. The Forest Stewardship Council (FSC) is the predominant standard. Family businesses may struggle to meet certification programs but can align themselves with the principles of practice.

Target 15.3 – Combating Desertification and Land Degradation

In regions affected by desertification and land degradation, family enterprises can play a crucial role in addressing these challenges. By adopting sustainable agricultural practices, such as water conservation techniques, soil management strategies and cultivating drought-resistant crops, they can mitigate the impacts of desertification and promote the restoration of degraded lands. However, these efforts are often hindered by limited access to resources, knowledge and technology, as well as the impacts of climate change exacerbating the severity and frequency of droughts and extreme weather events.

Target 15.4 – Conserving Mountain Ecosystems

For family businesses located near or operating in mountain regions, conserving mountain ecosystems and their biodiversity is a critical responsibility. They can support conservation efforts, implement sustainable tourism practices and promote the preservation of traditional knowledge and cultural practices related to mountain ecosystems (Geneletti & Dawa, 2009). By investing in sustainable infrastructure development and adopting environmentally friendly practices, these businesses can minimise their impact on these ecosystems. A major challenge for family businesses in these regions is balancing economic activities with environmental conservation, as many family businesses in mountain regions rely on natural resources for their livelihoods (Kreutzmann, 2024). Despite close links to the environment the constraints of finance and technology are a major challenge.

Target 15.5 – Protecting Biodiversity and Threatened Species

Safeguarding biodiversity and threatened species are a collective responsibility that family businesses can contribute to in various ways. These businesses can also raise awareness about the importance of biodiversity, collaborate with environmental organisations and encourage their employees and local communities to participate in conservation activities (Hajjar & Oldekop, 2018). Furthermore, they can support research and monitoring efforts and advocate for stronger policies and regulations to protect threatened species and their habitats.

Target 15.6 – Fair and Equitable Sharing of Genetic Resources

Family enterprises that utilise genetic resources or traditional knowledge must ensure fair and equitable sharing of benefits with local communities and Indigenous peoples. This can involve establishing benefit-sharing agreements, respecting intellectual property rights and promoting the sustainable use of these resources (Schroeder & Pogge, 2009). By fostering mutually beneficial relationships with local communities and Indigenous peoples, family enterprises can contribute to the preservation of traditional knowledge and the sustainable use of genetic resources, while also promoting social and economic development.

Target 15.7 – Combating Wildlife Trafficking

The illegal trade in wildlife products poses a significant threat to biodiversity and the survival of many species. Family businesses can take a stand against wildlife trafficking by implementing strict policies against the trade of illegal wildlife products, raising awareness among their employees and communities and supporting law enforcement efforts (Phelps et al., 2016). They can also collaborate with conservation organisations and government agencies to combat the demand and supply of illegal wildlife products (Zain, 2020). Tourism family businesses dependent on wildlife play a direct role in creating an alternative political economy as opposed to wildlife trade. Like other SDG#15 targets, family businesses should also adopt nature-related disclosure practices.

Target 15.8 – Preventing and Controlling Invasive Alien Species

Invasive alien species can have devastating impacts on native ecosystems, biodiversity and economic activities. Family enterprises can contribute to preventing and controlling these species by implementing biosecurity measures, supporting research and monitoring efforts, and promoting sustainable practices that minimise the introduction and spread of invasive species (Hulme, 2009). They can also collaborate with relevant authorities and organisations to develop and implement effective management strategies for invasive alien species. Like other SDG#15 targets, nature-related disclosure practices are also important for family businesses to embrace.

Target 15.9 – Integrating Biodiversity Values Into Planning and Strategies

To truly embrace sustainability, family enterprises must integrate biodiversity values into their planning, development processes and strategies. This can be achieved by conducting comprehensive environmental impact assessments, adopting sustainable business practices and considering the value of ecosystem services in their decision-making processes (Houdet, 2008). Through the implementation of these measures, family enterprises can play a significant role in advancing SDG#15 and contribute to the conservation and sustainable use of terrestrial ecosystems and biodiversity.

Family Business and an Eco-centric Approach to Biodiversity

Family businesses possess a distinct advantage in leading the transition from a human-centric to an eco-centric approach. Their deep-rooted connections to local communities and environments provide a natural foundation for this shift. While traditional Environmental, Social and Governance (ESG) metrics have primarily focused on promoting sustainable finance, green taxonomy screening and sustainability reporting, recent research underscores the urgency for greater accountability and action to counter species extinction – a challenge that family businesses are well-positioned to address.

The recent research by Miroshnychenko et al. (2024) examined the environmental management practices of family businesses concerning sustainability. Miroshnychenko et al. (2024) analysed 1,690 family and non-family publicly traded firms from 29 countries and 19 industries over the period 2007–2014. They found that there were substantial heterogeneity in the environmental practices of family firms, ranging from extremely unsustainable to highly sustainable. On the end of the pro-sustainable continuum, sustainable family businesses tended to be older and were smaller in size. They also found that many sustainable family businesses had independent directors and institutional ownership. High-income countries were also noted as having the highest rates of sustainable family business. This implies understanding the role of family business in biodiversity management and the achievement of SDG#15. Unsurprisingly, the study found that family businesses that were in 'dirty industries' (Manufacturing and fossil fuel-based industries) were not more sustainable than non-family businesses.

Family businesses with strong financial performance and a long-term outlook are more likely to become champions of environmental stewardship. Family businesses that have a strong long-term presence in local communities are more likely to have their operations and decision-making processes closely intertwined with the surrounding environment. This proximity to the natural world fosters a deeper understanding of the intricate relationships between business activities and ecological systems. SDG#15 is an important SDG for family businesses because sustainability in these businesses tend to have an anthropocentric bias, limiting their effectiveness in protecting biodiversity (Kopnina et al., 2024).

The Chapters and Contribution to SDG#15

This book showcases how family businesses contribute to preserving and sustainably managing terrestrial ecosystems, forests and biodiversity. A summary of the chapters in this book are provided below.

Chapter 2 provides an explanation of what family businesses are and how they contribute to global economies. Chapter 3 explores Bambra Agroforestry Farm which exemplifies how integrating forestry into agricultural landscapes can significantly contribute to SDG#15. The farm is owned and operated by Rowan and Claire Reid in Victoria, Australia and have demonstrated that commercial tree growing, and conventional agriculture can coexist. Through education, consultancy and practical demonstration, Bambra Agroforestry Farm has become a living laboratory, showcasing how farmers can adopt sustainable land management practices that promote the sustainable use of terrestrial ecosystems. The Reid family has planted over 50 commercial tree species and implemented various planting arrangements and regenerative management techniques. The business model is an inspiring example of how agricultural practices can be transformed to align with the goals of SDG#15.

The chapter on Echo Hills Farm, Chapter 4, showcases how the family-owned property in Queensland, Australia, contributes to SDG#15 through innovative regenerative agriculture practices. The Thompson family have owned the business for 75 years and have implemented a holistic approach to land management including managed grazing, water conservation and the integration of digital technologies to support sustainable farming practices. The Thompsons' commitment to SDG#15 is evident in their efforts to conserve and restore terrestrial ecosystems, restore degraded land and protect biodiversity and natural habitats. By transitioning from continuous cropping to regenerative practices, they have increased soil carbon levels, rehabilitated eroded areas and created a diverse landscape that supports native flora and fauna. The chapter also highlights the importance of community engagement, knowledge sharing and advocacy in promoting sustainable land management practices and shows how the Thompsons extend their impact beyond their farm to achieve SDG#15.

Chapter 5 brings us to Honduras and features the Paz family, who are the owners of Del Lago Orgánico. The family business creates a range of 100% natural products sourced from coffee, cacao, green plantain, sweet potato, cassava, taro and other ingredients. Their product line includes specialty coffee, coffee pulp and cacao husk infusions, gluten-free flours, cacao powder and sugar-free chocolate. All these items are internationally certified by The Vegan Society. Protecting the land and maintaining the biodiversity of the flora and fauna is core to the business operations of this family. The Paz family see the need to conserve and protect life on land and has organised their farm so that it has become a 'small lung' in the region. This chapter showcases how they have helped other farmers to commit themselves to SDG#15 through dialogue and education.

Chapter 6 explores how SSS Strawberries contributes to SDG#15 through its innovative and sustainable agricultural practices. The family-owned business is a leading Australian strawberry producer. The Dang family has implemented various strategies that align with SDG#15 targets, particularly focusing on sustainable land management, combating desertification, protecting biodiversity and integrating ecosystem values into their operations. SSS Strawberries employs sustainable farming practices such as organic methods, mulching, optimising irrigation and cover cropping to maintain soil health and prevent erosion. The company's commitment to biodiversity is evident in their integrated pest management approach, which reduces reliance on chemical interventions. They also collaborate with research institutions to develop resilient crop varieties and support local farmers in enhancing agricultural sustainability. The company showcases how a family business can contribute to SDG#15 through sustainable farming practices.

This next book chapter, Chapter 7, discusses SOILCO which is an Australian family-founded business with over 40 years of experience in organics recycling. This business contributes to SDG#15 by designing, building and operating innovative organics recycling facilities. The process used by this business diverts waste from landfills and supports soil regeneration, carbon sequestration and thus ecosystem resilience. A key feature of their business model is transforming organic waste into quality-assured compost and mulch products that regenerate soil health. They use a circular economy approach to organic waste management with particular use of their products in urban locations. SOILCO demonstrates how businesses in the waste management and soil improvement sectors can contribute to SDG#15, particularly in urban settings.

Chapter 8 features MyHive which is a sustainable beekeeping business in the United Arab Emirates (UAE). MyHive was founded by Alaa Mustafa and his brother Faris Saeed and operates within Dubai promoting biodiversity and sustainable beekeeping practices. MyHive's activities directly support several SDG#15 targets, including conservation and restoration of terrestrial ecosystems (SDG#15.1 and 15.2), and protect bees from extreme heat conditions and involve the local community in environmental protection. MyHive also provides free education through interactive apiary visits and beekeeping workshops. The chapter highlights how MyHive's business model aligns with SDG#15 by protecting indigenous bee species, promoting sustainable beekeeping practices and raising awareness about the importance of bees in the ecosystem.

The final chapter in the book, Chapter 9, is about the Emiliana Vineyard which is a pioneering example of sustainable wine production in Chile. Emiliana Vineyard is owned by the Guilisasti family and demonstrates how a family business can drive innovation and environmental stewardship in the wine sector. As the largest organic winery globally, Emiliana Vineyard has made significant contributions to achieving SDG#15 (Life on Land) through its organic and biodynamic farming practices. The vineyard's commitment to sustainable ecosystem management and biodiversity promotion aligns closely with SDG#15's targets. The practices enforced by the Guilisasti family at Emiliana Vineyard, such as avoiding synthetic fertilisers and pesticides, implementing composting techniques and creating habitats for diverse species have set the standards for sustainable viticulture in Chile and internationally. The Guilisasti family's vision led to a 10-year plan that transformed the Emiliana Vineyard into an organic and biodynamic winery, demonstrating that high-quality wines can be produced while enhancing environmental management. The company's commitment extends beyond environmental concerns to include social responsibility initiatives.

Conclusion

Family businesses have a pivotal role to play in achieving SDG#15, Life on Land. With their deep roots in local communities and close connections to the natural environment, family firms are uniquely positioned to contribute to the protection, restoration and sustainable use of terrestrial ecosystems. Their long-term outlook and commitment to ethical practices provide a solid foundation for promoting sustainable land management practices, combating desertification and halting biodiversity loss.

The book series, which employs a case-based approach, provides evidence of the role of family businesses in effectively contributing to all SDGs. Each book in the 17-volume series comprises a set of short, easy-to-read family business cases related to the unique SDG being discussed. This format allows the works to be accessible not only to academics but also to family business practitioners, owners, advisors, policy-makers, NGOs, business associations, philanthropic centres and those with a general interest in entrepreneurship and business. By showcasing real-world examples, the book series highlights the potential of family businesses to contribute to the achievement of SDG#15, Life on Land.

References

Convention on Biological Diversity. (2022). *Kunming-Montreal global biodiversity framework*. Convention on Biological Diversity. https://www.cbd.int/article/cop15-final-text-kunming-montreal-gbf-221222

Geneletti, D., & Dawa, D. (2009). Environmental impact assessment of mountain tourism in developing regions: A study in Ladakh, Indian Himalaya. *Environmental Impact Assessment Review*, *29*(4), 229–242. https://doi.org/10.1016/j.eiar.2008.02.002

Global Reporting Initiative. (2019). *Integrating SDGs into sustainability reporting*. Global Reporting Initiative. https://www.globalreporting.org/public-policy/sustainable-development/integrating-sdgs-into-sustainability-reporting/

Hajjar, R., & Oldekop, J. A. (2018). Research frontiers in community forest management. *Current Opinion in Environmental Sustainability*, *32*, 119–125. https://doi.org/10.1016/j.cosust.2018.06.003

Houdet, J. (2008). *Integrating biodiversity into business strategies. The biodiversity accountability framework*. FRB–Orée.

Hulme, P. E. (2009). Trade, transport and trouble: Managing invasive species pathways in an era of globalization. *Journal of Applied Ecology*, *46*(1), 10–18. https://doi.org/10.1111/j.1365-2664.2008.01600.x

Kopnina, H., Zhang, Y., Anthony, C., Hassan, Z., & Maroun, M. (2024). Ecocentric accounting for biodiversity in family businesses. *Journal of Cleaner Production*, 123456. https://doi.org/10.1016/j.jclepro.2024.123456

Krause, M. S., Droste, N., & Matzdorf, B. (2020). What makes businesses commit to nature conservation? *Business Strategy and the Environment*, *30*(2), 741–755. https://doi.org/10.1002/bse.2650

Kreutzmann, H. (2024). Common challenges and differing responses: Reflections about sustainable mountain development. *Global Environmental Research*, *27*(2), 81–90.

Miroshnychenko, I., Miller, D., De Massis, A., & Le Breton-Miller, I. (2024). Are family firms green? *Small Business Economics*. https://doi.org/10.1007/s11187-024-00907-1

Phelps, J., Biggs, D., & Webb, E. L. (2016). Tools and terms for understanding illegal wildlife trade. *Frontiers in Ecology and the Environment*, *14*(9), 479–489. https://doi.org/10.1002/fee.1325

Schroeder, D., & Pogge, T. (2009). Incentives for access to the benefits of bioprospecting. In *Incentives for global public health* (pp. 141–158). Cambridge University Press.

Science Based Targets Network. (n.d.). *Science based targets for nature (SBTN)*. Science Based Targets Network. https://sciencebasedtargetsnetwork.org/

Taskforce on Nature-related Financial Disclosures. (n.d.). *Taskforce on nature-related financial disclosures*. Taskforce on Nature-related Financial Disclosures. https://tnfd.global/

United Nations. (2021). *The 17 goals*. United Nations. https://sdgs.un.org/goals

United Nations. (n.d.). *SDG indicators: Global indicator framework for the sustainable development goals and targets of the 2030 agenda for sustainable development.* United Nations. https://unstats.un.org/sdgs/indicators/indicators-list/

United Nations Global Compact. (n.d.). *The SDGs explained for business.* United Nations Global Compact. https://unglobalcompact.org/sdgs/about

Zain, S. (2020). Combating wildlife trafficking from the consumer perspective. *Journal of Scandinavian Studies in Criminology and Crime Prevention*, *21*(1), 2–18. https://doi.org/10.1080/14043858.2020.1727481

Chapter 2

Roots of Success: The Impact of Family Businesses on Economies and Society

Naomi Birdthistle

Griffith University, Australia

What Does It Mean to Be a Family Business?

The study of family businesses is an emerging field in academia. However, defining what constitutes a family business remains a significant challenge. Davis, a renowned expert in this area, has meticulously reviewed existing literature and categorised definitions into two main types: structural definitions and process definitions (Davis, 2001). Structural definitions focus on ownership and management arrangements, such as owning 51% or more of the business, while process definitions emphasise the family's engagement and influence in business operations. Table 2.1 highlights varying perspectives from influential researchers, providing insight into the multifaceted approaches used to define family businesses.

Table 2.1. Definitions of Family Businesses With a Structural or Process Lens Applied.

Family Business Definition	Author	Structural or Process Lens Applied
Members of one family own enough voting equity to control strategy, policy and tactical implementation	Miller and Rice (1967)	Process definition
Ownership control by a single family or individual	Barnes and Hershon (1976)	Structural definition

(Continued)

Attaining the 2030 Sustainable Development Goal of Life on Land, 13–26
Copyright © 2025 Naomi Birdthistle
Published under exclusive licence by Emerald Publishing Limited
doi:10.1108/978-1-83608-212-520241002

Table 2.1. *(Continued)*

Family Business Definition	Author	Structural or Process Lens Applied
Two or more family members influence the direction of the business through the exercise of management roles, kinship ties or ownership rights	Davis and Tagiuri (1982)	Process definition
Family influence over business decisions	Dyer (1986)	Process definition
Ownership and operation by members of one or two families	Stern (1986)	Structural definition
Legal control over the business by family members	Lansberg et al. (1988)	Structural definition
Closely identified with at least two generations of a family, the link has had a mutual influence on the company policy and the interests and objectives of the family	Donnelley (1964)	Process definition
Expectation or actuality of succession by a family member	Churchill and Hatten (1987)	Process definition
Single-family effectively controls the firm through the ownership of greater than 50% of the voting shares and a significant portion of the firm's senior management team is drawn from the same family	Leach et al. (1990)	A mix of structural and process definitions

In their study, Astrachan and Shanker (2003, p. 211) highlight the lack of a universally accepted, concise definition for family businesses. Consequently, they created a spectrum to define family businesses, spanning from broad to narrow (see Fig. 2.1). This spectrum captures varying levels of family engagement in business, offering different degrees of specificity in defining family businesses:

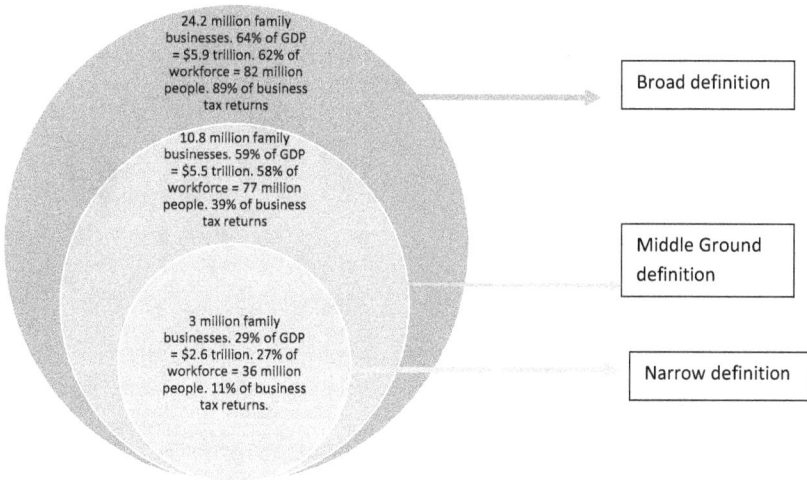

Fig. 2.1.   Defining Family Business: The Family Business Bull's-Eye.
Source: Adapted from: Astrachan and Shanker (2003, p. 218).

- Broad Definition: At the outer edge, family participation influences strategic direction. Even with minimal family involvement, it qualifies as a family business.
- Middle Ground Definition: Closer to the centre, this emphasises passing the business to a family member. Incumbents actively manage, preparing for generational transition.
- Narrow Definition: At the core, extensive family involvement spans generations, including siblings, cousins and younger relatives in various roles.

The diverse definitions within the bull's eye spectrum highlight the challenge of precisely defining family businesses. Due to their varying nature and the absence of universally agreed-upon criteria, Astrachan and Shanker's spectrum recognises different levels of family involvement. This nuanced approach allows for a deeper understanding of the term and its implications. Additionally, Pieper et al. (2021) builds upon Astrachan and Shanker's bullseye model, as shown in Fig. 2.2, applying it to United States (US) family businesses across different time periods, revealing the growth in their volume.

In contrast to the Astrachan and Shanker (2003) study findings, Pieper et al. (2021) found that in relation to the 'Broad' circle there is a small reduction in results, i.e. the decreased contribution of small businesses to gross domestic product (GDP) and workshop. Therefore, small businesses have grown slower than larger businesses in the last 18 years in the US. In the narrow ring, they have found that some large family businesses may have decreased percentage contributions to GDP and workforce. For example, Walmart would qualify to be considered in the narrow ring.

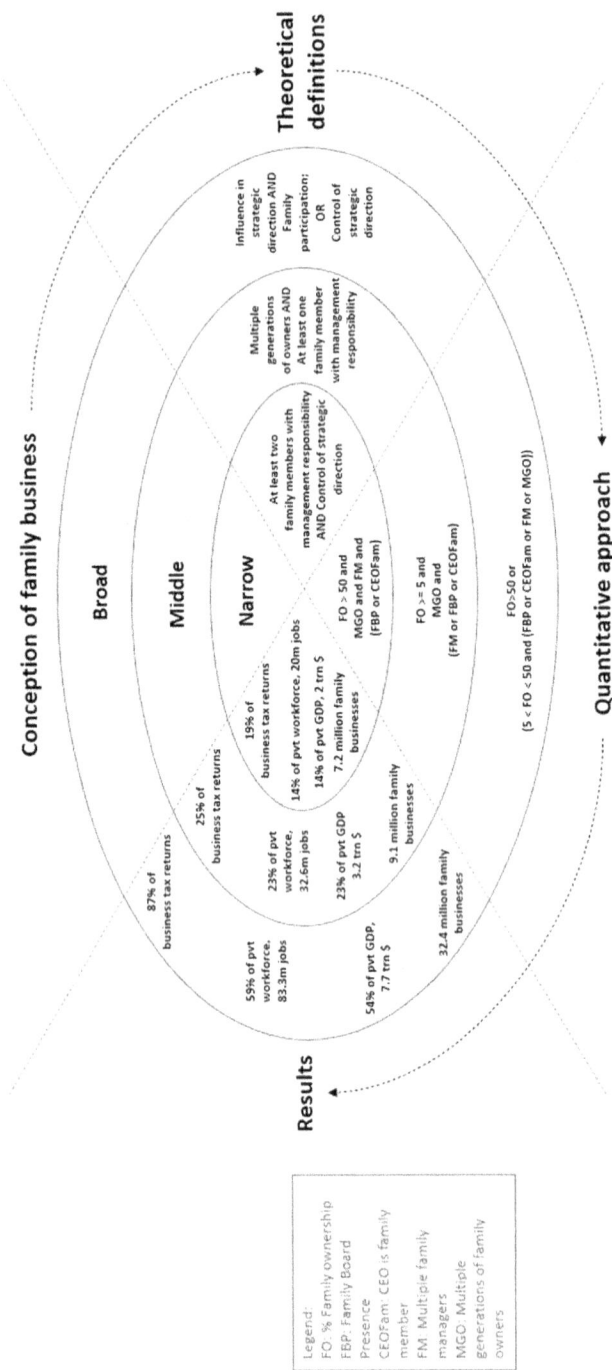

Fig. 2.2.   Bullseye 2021. *Source: Pieper et al. (2021, p. 15).*

The absence of a universally agreed-upon definition for family businesses has led to diverse interpretations among writers and researchers. This lack of consensus raises concerns, potentially affecting research outcomes. Cano-Rubio et al. (2017) advocate for a single general criterion to ensure consistent and comparable results. The absence of standardisation also highlights a gap in field discussions, emphasising the need for dialogue. Some writers use 'family business' ambiguously, hindering comprehensive understanding. Differentiating family businesses from other enterprises is crucial, considering their wide spectrum – from local small enterprises to global giants, like LG and Bacardi. Notably, family businesses can be privately owned or publicly traded (e.g. CBS & Viacom).

To address these complexities, the authors selected self-identified family businesses and categorised them using structural or process definitions (as proposed by Davis, 2001). Their systematic approach contributes to understanding this vital sector.

Key Characteristics of a Family Business

Family businesses are not homogenous entities, and their characteristics can vary significantly based on various factors. The size, industry, culture and level of family involvement all contribute to the uniqueness of each family business. As a result, these businesses may face distinct challenges related to family dynamics, succession planning and finding a balance between personal and professional interests. Despite these differences, family businesses play an integral and diverse role in the global business landscape, making substantial contributions to economies worldwide. Being a family business implies that ownership, control and management primarily rest in the hands of one or multiple family members. These family members have a direct say in decision-making processes and significantly influence the company's strategic direction and operations. The family members in this context are typically those related by blood or marriage.

Several key characteristics distinguish family businesses, including active family involvement in the business, significant family ownership, a long-term orientation with a focus on legacy and continuity and the influence of family values and culture. Succession planning is also crucial to ensure smooth transitions of leadership and ownership between generations. Family businesses often prioritise relationships with employees and customers, fostering loyalty and trust. Moreover, family businesses may have family members assuming multiple roles, taking on responsibilities as both family members and business professionals, creating a unique organizational dynamic. In summary, the diverse nature of family businesses contributes to their resilience and adaptability in navigating challenges and opportunities, making them an important and enduring presence in the business world.

Family Businesses Around the World

Family businesses are undeniably a reality rather than an enigma. In fact, they are the most common ownership model found across the world and hold significant influence over the global economy. Their prevalence and contributions to GDP are immense and well-documented. The impact of family businesses on the global economy is not to be underestimated. Their longevity, adaptability and dedication to long-term sustainability are factors that have enabled them to thrive and make substantial contributions to economic growth and prosperity. As a result, family businesses are a vital and enduring aspect of the business landscape, and their presence and influence are felt across continents and industries. As per Tharawat Magazine (2023), Fig. 2.3 highlights the substantial contributions that family businesses make to global GDP. These data underscore their economic significance and the essential role they play in various industries and markets worldwide.

It is evident from the research produced by Tharawat Magazine (2023) that family businesses play a significant and important role in the economies of various nations and have cemented their impact on a nation's GDP, highlighting their enduring importance in the business landscape. In India, for example, family businesses contributed to a remarkable 79% of the country's GDP, and it is home to 15 of the world's largest 500 family businesses (Tharawat Magazine, 2023). This substantial contribution demonstrates the enduring strength and influence of family businesses in one of the world's largest economies. Similarly, in the United Arab Emirates (UAE), family businesses have a substantial presence, accounting for an estimated 70% of employment. Their significant representation further illustrates their role as a driving force in the UAE economy (Tharawat Magazine, 2023).

Family-owned businesses indeed play a significant role in the global economy. According to the 2023 EY and University of St. Gallen Family Business Index, the largest family enterprises are growing faster than the global economy, with a remarkable 10% increase in revenue compared to their 2021 findings. These family businesses collectively generated an astounding $8.02 trillion in revenue (EY Global, 2023). Let's take a closer look at some notable examples:

> Wal-Mart: Owned by the Waltons, Wal-Mart recorded impressive revenues of $572.8 billion in 2022. The company's global operations employed 2.3 million people, highlighting its substantial impact on job creation. (Walmart, 2023)

> Volkswagen: The Porsche family's ownership of Volkswagen has been pivotal to the automotive giant's success. In 2021, Volkswagen's total revenues reached $18.8 billion, contributing significantly to the overall market revenue of $1.8 trillion for the same year. (Statista Mobility Market Insights, 2022)

These examples highlight the resilience, adaptability and long-term vision of family-owned businesses, allowing them to thrive and contribute significantly to global economic prosperity. Their ability to build enduring brands and drive substantial revenue reaffirms their position as key players in the global business

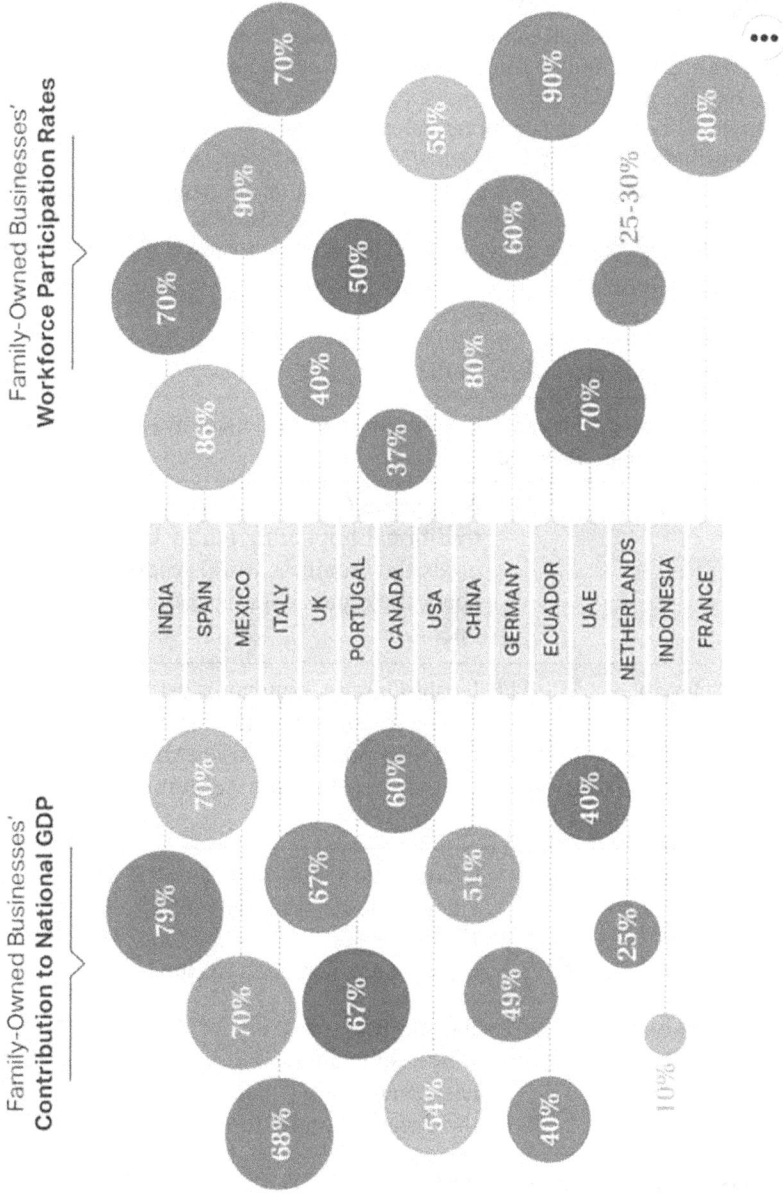

Fig. 2.3. Global Assessment of Family-Owned Businesses: National GDP Contribution and Workforce Participation. *Source:* Tharawat Magazine (2023, para. 5).

landscape. Family businesses have a long history in some countries, deeply ingrained in the fabric of their economies. For instance, the Osaka temple-builder Kongo Gumi held the title of the world's oldest family business, established way back in 578 (McClathchie, 2023). Although it ceased operations in 2006, it was replaced by Nishiyama Onsen Keiunkan which has had 52 generations of the same family operating the family business. Some of the oldest family businesses in the world can be seen in Table 2.2.

These examples underscore the enduring influence of family-owned businesses, significantly contributing to global economic activity and shaping commercial landscapes across diverse industries and regions. Research findings emphasise their ongoing impact on national economies, driven by adaptability, innovation and contributions to growth. As we peer into the future, family businesses remain pivotal in shaping economies and societies worldwide.

Table 2.2. Oldest Family Businesses in the World.

Family Business	Country of Origin	Year Founded	Functions of the Family Business
Nishiyama Onsen Keiunkan	Japan	705 AD	Nishiyama Onsen Keiunkan is a traditional hot spring inn in Japan. It holds the Guinness world record for being the oldest hotel in continuous operation.
Hoshi Onsen Chojukan	Japan	718 AD	Hoshi Onsen Chojukan is a traditional Japanese hot spring inn located in the Ishikawa prefecture. It is currently being led by the 46th generation of the Hoshi family.
Château de Goulaine	France	1000	Château de Goulaine is a castle and vineyard located in the Loire Valley France. It has been in the Goulaine family since it was established.
Barone Ricasoli	Italy	1141	Barone Ricasoli is one of the oldest wineries in Italy and is in Tuscany. It has remained under the ownership of the Ricasoli family for over 850 years
Richard de Bas	France	1326	Richard de Bas is a paper mill located in Ambert France. It has been operated by the Bas family for over 700 years and is known for producing high-quality handmade papers.

Table 2.2. *(Continued)*

Family Business	Country of Origin	Year Founded	Functions of the Family Business
Antinori	Italy	1385	Antinori is another renowned winery in Tuscany Italy. It is one of the oldest family-run businesses specialising in wine production.
Rentez-Vous	France	1394	Rentez-Vous is a French clothing business that has been passed down through generations of the Rentez family for more than 600 years.
Zildjian	Turkey/ USA	1623	Zildjian is renowned for manufacturing cymbals. The business was established in Turkey and later moved to the US. It has remained family-owned for nearly 400 years.
Kikkoman	Japan	1630	Kikkoman is a well-known Japanese food company specialising in soy sauce and other condiments. It has been owned by the Mogi family for over 360 years.

Source: Author's own.

Countries Represented in This Book

The family businesses portrayed in this book come from Australia, Honduras, Chile and the UAE.

Australia's business landscape is rich with family enterprises. Evidence suggests that family businesses constitute approximately 70% of all businesses in the country (CoSpedia, 2022). Family Business Australia (n.d.) reports that these businesses contribute over AUS$4.3 trillion to the economy, with an average annual turnover of AUS$12 million. Notably, family businesses also feature prominently among the top 500 private companies in Australia (IBISWorld, 2022). Upon closer examination, the top 26 companies include 10 family-owned businesses, with three of the top five also being family businesses. Australia boasts a heritage of longstanding family businesses, with the oldest being founded in 1808, Summerville farm in Tasmania's Derwent Valley and is being led by the seventh generation of the family. Other old businesses that are still being run by members of the founding family include Lionel Samson & Son which was founded in 1829 by two brothers who came to the Swan

River Colony on one of the first settlement vessels. In the 1880s, Lionel Samson and Son was the single largest importer of beers and spirits into Australia. Coopers Beer is a family run business, which was established in Adelaide in 1862, and they are still pouring pints around the country. Another brewery that is family owned is J. Furphy & Sons, which is a fifth generation, family-owned manufacturing business based in Shepparton, Northern Victoria and with operations in Albury NSW and Geelong Victoria. Phillip Blashki migrated from England and established the firm P. Blashki & Sons around 1875. The family business still operates in the 21st century, making regalia including academic gowns, judges' wigs, chains of office, medals, badges, epaulettes and swords. Peacock Bros. was established on Collins Street in Melbourne, 1888. Brothers Ernest and Charles Peacock founded the small general printing business together, quickly developing a reputation for exceptional quality and outstanding service.

Honduras, located in Central America, has faced challenges such as military rule, corruption, poverty and crime. Despite these difficulties, it remains a vibrant and diverse country with a rich cultural heritage (BBC News, 2023). With a population of 9.4 million, Honduras has a nominal GDP of $32 billion in 2022, and it is classified as a low/middle-income country (World Bank Group, 2024). Approximately, 60% of its population lives in poverty (International Trade Administration, 2024). The country has experienced moderate economic growth since 2010, with an average growth rate of 3.8% in the three years before COVID-19 (International Trade Administration, 2024). The economy is primarily based on agriculture, which contributes 14% to its GDP. Coffee is the leading export, accounting for 22% of total export revenues (Wikipedia, 2024). According to Discua-Cruz et al. (2023), most businesses in Honduras take the form of family firms and research has indicated that these enterprises are predominantly led by men. Honduras is recognised as the world's leading coffee producer and according to Mercanta (n.d.) over 100,000 small-scale family farms rely on coffee for their livelihood. BUFETE CASCO-LIC is Honduras' oldest law firm that specialises in intellectual property. Members of the Casco family have been running the family business for more than 110 years (Casco, n.d.), and currently, three members of the Casco family are actively involved in the leadership of the family business.

Family businesses play a significant role in Chile's economy. According to the Global Family Business Index produced by EY and the University of St. Gallen, Chile has six of its family businesses listed in the top 500 family businesses in the world (Bnamericas, 2019). Those six include

(1) Copec Companies in 77th place,
(2) Antarchile in 81st place,
(3) Cencosud in 99th place,
(4) SACI Falabella in 127th place,
(5) Queneco in 261st place and
(6) CMPC in 320th place.

These businesses had combined revenues of US$84,210 million. Other notable statistics include family businesses make up 44% of the listed companies in Chile and 49.6% of small- and medium-sized companies are family owned (Briano-Turrent et al., 2020). Watkins-Fassler et al. (2016) note the contributions made by family-owned businesses in Chile and they include making up 70% of the GDP and they generate approximately 60% of employment. One of the oldest family businesses in Chile is Lingues hacienda, established in 1760, where Lingues has been in the same family for more than four centuries (Müller & Sandoval-Arzaga, 2021).

In the United Arab Emirates (UAE), approximately 343,000 private sector businesses, including family enterprises, significantly contribute to the national economy (Puri-Mirza, 2021). According to Abbas (2022), family-owned businesses account for 70% of the UAE's GDP. The National (2023) reports that up to 90% of private companies in the country are family businesses, employing over 70% of the sector's workforce. Forbes Middle East ranks 21 UAE families among the Arab world's 100 most powerful family businesses, second only to Saudi Arabia (Varghese, 2021). Recognising their importance, Sheikh Mohammed bin Rashid, Vice President and Ruler of Dubai, actively promotes family business growth. He established a centre dedicated to scaling and supporting family enterprises, aiming to double their number by 2032 and potentially boost the GDP to $320 billion (Cabral, 2022).

The Future of Family Businesses Post-COVID-19

During the COVID-19 pandemic, family businesses demonstrated a notable level of resilience compared to non-family businesses. Research conducted by Bajpai et al. (2021) on a global scale revealed that family businesses laid off fewer staff (8.5%) compared to non-family businesses (10.2%). This ability to retain more employees during challenging times highlights the resilience and adaptability of family businesses in the face of economic disruptions caused by the pandemic.

Due to their capacity to weather crises and make strategic decisions with a long-term perspective, Bajpai et al. (2021) argue that family businesses are positioned to play a significant role in driving the global economic recovery from COVID-19 pandemic. As the world continues to recover from the impacts of the pandemic, family businesses may emerge as key drivers of economic growth and stability, both at the local and global levels. The findings of this research suggest that family businesses' unique characteristics, such as strong family values, commitment to employees and focus on long-term sustainability, contributed to their ability to navigate the challenges brought about by the pandemic more effectively than other companies. As a result, they are expected to be instrumental in fostering economic recovery and rebuilding in the post-pandemic era.

References

Abbas, W. (2022, September 19). UAE: New initiative to turn 200 family businesses into major companies by 2023. *Khaleej Times.* https://www.khaleejtimes.com/business/uae-new-initiative-to-turn-200-family-businesses-into-major-companies-by-2030

Astrachan, J. H., & Shanker, M. C. (2003, September). Family businesses' contribution to the U.S. economy: A closer look. *Family Business Review, 16*(3), 211–219.

Bajpai, A., Calabro, A., & McGinness, T. (2021). *Mastering a comeback: How family businesses are triumphing over COVID-19.* KPMG.

Barnes, L. B., & Hershon, S. A. (1976). Transferring power in the family business. *Harvard Business Review, 54*(4), 105–114.

BBC News. (2023). Honduras country profile. *BBC News.* https://www.bbc.com/news/world-latin-america-18954311

Bnamericas. (2019). Four Chilean firms rise in the ranking of the 500 largest family businesses in the world. *Bnamericas.* https://www.bnamericas.com/en/news/four-chilean-firms-rise-in-the-ranking-of-the-500-largest-family-businesses-in-the-world

Briano-Turrent, G., Watkins-Fassler, K., & Puente-Esparza, M. (2020). The effect of the board composition on dividends: The case of Brazilian and Chilean family firms. *European Journal of Family Business, 10,* 43–60.

Cabral, A. (2022). New UAE initiative aims to double family businesses' contribution to GDP to $320 bn by 2032. *The National.* https://www.thenationalnews.com/business/economy/2022/09/19/new-uae-initiative-aims-to-double-family-businesses-contribution-to-gdp-to-320bn-by-2032/

Cano-Rubio, M., Fuentes-Lombardo, G., & Vallejo-Martos, M. C. (2017). Influence of the lack of a standard definition of "family business" on researcher into their international strategies. *European Research on Management and Business Economics, 23,* 132–146.

Casco. (n.d.). Our Firm. *Bufete Casco.* https://cascomark.com/about/

Churchill, N. C., & Hatten, K. J. (1987). Non-market-based transfers of wealth and power: A research framework for family businesses. *American Journal of Small Business, 11*(3), 51–64.

CoSpedia. (2022). Why family businesses are the backbone of the Australian economy. *CoSpedia.* https://www.cos.net.au/c/cospedia/family-business-australian-economy

Davis, J. (2001, July). *Definitions and typologies of the family business.* Harvard Business School. Background Note, 802-007.

Davis, J., & Tagiuri, R. (1982). *The influence of life stages on father-son work relationships in family companies.* Unpublished manuscript. Graduate School of Business Administration, University of Southern California.

Discua-Cruz, A., Hamilton, E., Campopiano, G., & Jack, S. (2023, October 17). Women show their strengths when family businesses are in trouble. *FamilyBusiness.org.* https://familybusiness.org/content/women-show-their-strengths-when-family-businesses-are-in-trouble

Donnelley, R. (1964). The family business. *Harvard Business Review, 42*(4), 93–105.

Dyer, W. G., Jr. (1986). *Cultural changes in family business: Anticipating and managing business and family transitions.* Jossey-Bass.

EY Global. (2023). How the largest family enterprises are outstripping global economic growth. *EY Global.* https://www.ey.com/en_gl/insights/family-enterprise/family-business-index

IBISWorld. (2022). Australia's top 500 private companies in 2022. *IBISWorld.* https://www.ibisworld.com/blog/top-500-private-companies-2022/61/1133/

International Trade Administration. (2024). Honduras – Country commercial guide: Market overview. *International Trade Administration.* https://www.trade.gov/country-commercial-guides/honduras-market-overview

Lansberg, I. S., Perrow, E. L., & Rogolsky, S. (1988). Family business as an emerging field. *Family Business Review, 1*(1), 1–8.

Leach, P., Kenway-Smith, W., Hart, A., Morris, T., Ainsworth, J., Beterlsen, E., Iraqi, S., & Pasari, V. (1990). *Managing the family business in the UK. A Stoy Hayward survey in conjunction with the London Business School.* Stoy Hayward.

McClathchie, C. (2023, November 23). Why Japan is home to the world's oldest businesses. *CEO Magazine.* https://www.theceomagazine.com/business/management-leadership/japan-oldest-businesses/

Mercanta. (n.d.). Honduras. *Mercanta.* https://coffeehunter.com/our-origins/honduras/

Miller, E. J., & Rice, A. K. (1967). *Systems of organizations.* Tavistock.

Müller, C. & Sandoval-Arzaga, F. (2021). The syncretism (the first wave): The first family business in the region. In C. Müller, & F. Sandoval-Arzaga (Eds.), *Family business heterogeneity in Latin America.* Palgrave Studies in Family Business Heterogeneity (pp. 25-47). Palgrave Macmillan. https://doi.org/10.1007/978-3-030-78931-2_3

Pieper, T., Kellermanns, F., & Astrachan, J. (2021). Update 2021: Family businesses' contribution to the U.S. economy. *Family Enterprise.* https://familyenterpriseusa.com/wp-content/uploads/2021/02/FEUSA-2021-Study-Brochure_digital-v3.pdf

Puri-Mirza, A. (2021). Private sector establishments numbers UAE 2016-2020. *Statista.* https://www.statista.com/statistics/1148078/uae-number-of-private-sector-establishments/#:~:text=In%202020%2C%20the%20total%20number,compared%20to%20the%20previous%20year

Statista Mobility Market Insights. (2022). Porche report 2022. https://www.statista.com/study/60891/porsche-report/

Stern, M. H. (1986). *Inside the family-held business.* Harcourt Brace Jovanovich.

Tharawat Magazine. (2023, October 12). Economic impact of family businesses – A compilation of facts. *Tharawat Magazine Orbis Terra Media.* https://www.tharawat-magazine.com/facts/economic-impact-family-businesses/

The National. (2023, March 25). Sheikh Mohammed establishes centre to support family businesses in Dubai. *The National.* https://www.thenationalnews.com/uae/government/2023/02/02/sheikh-mohammed-establishes-centre-to-support-family-businesses-in-dubai/

Varghese, J. (2021). UAE: How did family businesses come about and how are they structured? Family business play a huge role in the Gulf region – But how do they operate? *Your Money.* https://gulfnews.com/your-money/expert-columns/uae-how-did-family-businesses-come-about-and-how-are-they-structured-1.1619001837624

Walmart. (2023). How many people work at Walmart? *Walmart.* https://corporate.walmart.com/askwalmart/how-many-people-work-at-walmart

Watkins-Fassler, K., Fernández-Pérez, V., & Rodríguez-Ariza, L. (2016). President interlocking, family firms and performance during turbulent times: Evidence from Latin America. *European Journal of Family Business*, *6*, 63–74. http://doi.org/10.1016/j.ejfb.2016.12.001

Wikipedia. (2024). Economy of Honduras. *Wikipedia*. https://en.wikipedia.org/wiki/Economy_of_Honduras

World Bank Group. (2024). The world bank in Honduras. *World Bank Group*. https://www.worldbank.org/en/country/honduras/overview

Chapter 3

Australia: A Forester Among Farmers – How Agriculture and Forestry Can Work Together to Save the Planet

Rosemary L. Fisher[a] *and Michael J. A. Seidler*[b]

[a]Swinburne University, Australia
[b]Greyhill Associates, Australia

Can cutting down trees help save the environment? Rowan Reid believed it could and set out to find a new way to approach the environmental, social and productivity limits of our conventional agriculture systems by integrating forestry into the agricultural landscape. In so doing, the Reid's family business contributes directly to achieving Sustainable Development Goal (SDG) 15: protect, restore and promote sustainable use of terrestrial ecosystems, sustainably manage forests, combat desertification and halt and reverse land degradation and halt biodiversity loss (United Nations, n.d.).

This family business developed and now demonstrates and disseminates the theory and practice of a way to manage land that makes good business sense to farmers. In so doing, the Reids have pioneered a way forward for Australian family business farmers to farm their lands in a commercially viable and environmentally beneficial way that has the potential to address the historic loss of vegetation that made Australia one of the top 10 deforestation hotspots in the world (Bush Heritage Australia, 2023).

> ...I could clearly see that commercial forestry, the act of planting trees for profit, could be made an attractive option for Australian farming families, but that the reasons, means products and markets would need to change. Forestry on farms would look different from what government and industry were doing. (Reid, 2019, p. 18)

Attaining the 2030 Sustainable Development Goal of Life on Land, 27–40
Copyright © 2025 Rosemary L. Fisher and Michael J. A. Seidler
Published under exclusive licence by Emerald Publishing Limited
doi:10.1108/978-1-83608-212-520241003

Introduction

Nestled in the picturesque countryside of Victoria, Australia, Bambra Agroforestry Farm stands as a testament to innovation and environmental sustainability. Owned and operated by Rowan and Claire Reid, this micro-family business has become a shining example of how cutting down trees can save the environment. In their quest to find an alternative approach to conventional agriculture systems limitations, Rowan Reid embarked on a journey that could revolutionise farmers' agricultural practices.

Recognising the urgent need to address environmental, social and productivity challenges within agriculture, Rowan set out to develop an approach that was economically viable. It would also contribute directly to rehabilitating and maintaining ecosystems degraded by conventional farming practices.

Although this work began nearly three decades before the establishment of the United Nations' Sustainable Development Goals (UNSDGs), the direct linkage to the principles underpinning SDG#15 is clear: Protect, restore and promote sustainable use of terrestrial ecosystems, sustainably manage forests, combat desertification and halt and reverse land degradation and halt biodiversity loss (United Nations, n.d., para. 1).

The vision was clear – to create a sustainable model that harmoniously combines agriculture and forestry, enhancing biodiversity, conserving the environment and reversing the devastating effects of land degradation brought about by 'traditional' farming practices.

With the goal of addressing Australia's status as one of the top 10 deforestation hotspots in the world (Bush Heritage Australia, 2023), the Reid family business has developed and disseminated a theory and practice that resonates with farmers. They have pioneered a way forward for Australian farmers to farm their lands in a commercially viable manner. This is while simultaneously addressing historic vegetation loss. By demonstrating how to integrate trees and shrubs back into the farming landscape, Bambra Agroforestry Farm offers a solution that makes practical business sense. It also helps combat deforestation and promotes sustainable land management.

Bambra Agroforestry Farm's innovative practices have not only transformed their own land but garnered attention and recognition from the broader agricultural community. Farmers across Australia have embraced the idea that commercial forestry and commercial agriculture is not mutually exclusive but complementary. Through the dissemination of their knowledge, Rowan and Claire Reid have inspired a new generation of farmers to rethink their land management practices. They have encouraged them to embrace agroforestry as a viable and sustainable path forward.

In addition to the practical implementation of their ideas, the Reid family has also dedicated themselves to spreading their message. They have also educated stakeholders about the benefits of integrating trees into farming systems. Rowan's commitment to communication and knowledge sharing has allowed him to build partnerships with research organisations, government agencies and the farming community at large. By effectively communicating the value proposition of agroforestry and its potential to address environmental challenges, Rowan seeks to build coalitions and influence policy discussions. In addition, he seeks to garner broader support for this cause.

As the case study of Bambra Agroforestry Farm unfolds, we will delve deeper into the key components of their business model, the resources that drive their success, their organizational structure and the challenges they face in achieving their goals. We will explore their communication strategies, commitment to SDG#15 and successes thus far. Through their story, we hope to inspire and empower postgraduate students and professionals alike, demonstrating the transformative potential of sustainable land management practices and the critical role that agroforestry can play in shaping a more sustainable future for agriculture in Australia and beyond.

Background to Bambra Agroforestry Farm

> Penetrating next through a narrow strip of casuarinae scrub, we found the remains of native huts; and beyond this scrub, we crossed a beautiful plain, covered with shining verdure and ornamented with trees, which, although 'dropped in nature's careless haste', gave the country the appearance of an extensive park (Mitchell, 1838, p. 90).

In many countries around the world, and Australia is no exception, trees – especially indigenous trees – have traditionally been seen as antithetical to agriculture. For many generations and in a variety of places, clearing the land of all native vegetation was seen as a necessary pre-requisite to efficient, 'modern' agriculture. As an example of this philosophy, at various times in Australia's history since British settlement, schemes that allocated crown land to settlers[1] required recipients to improve the land by preparing for agricultural use. The simplest improvement recognised was the clearing of all native vegetation – trees, shrubs and grasses.

> In 1861, the newly formed government of Australia passed the Crown Lands Alienation Act, which was designed to 'open up' the colony to settlement. Over the following century, that single Act effectively guaranteed the rapid clearing of vegetation by unrestricted settlement, for it penalized entitled landholders, via a forfeit to the Crown, for failing to 'develop' their lands. (Braithwaite, 1996, p. 111)

---

[1]Originally free settlers and emancipated convicts and later, post WWI and WWII, returned soldiers received land with this stipulation.

Today, it is now well understood that indigenous plants grow and prosper where they do because they are ideally suited to that particular environment. In addition, they play a vital role in maintaining that environment's balance. Wholesale removal leads to catastrophic consequences:

> As in many parts of Australia, the subsoils beneath the slightly undulating country of the Carnamah area are rich in salts. Settlers replaced native trees, shrubs and grasses – a plant community able to hold and use water efficiently – with bare, cultivated earth and short rooted annual crops. Water seeped below and brought destructive salts to the surface. Returned soldier Tom White and his wife Hilda called their Carnamah district farm 'Rosedale'. As the decades passed, clearing and cropping on Rosedale had unfortunate consequences. The creek running past the homestead turned saline, and any trees remaining beside the waterway sickened and died. (National Museum of Australia, 2022, para 14–15)

Despite this knowledge, the perception that forestry and traditional agriculture are mutually exclusive persists in many circles, contributing to ongoing land degradation and erosion issues (Evans, 2016; Williams et al., 2021).

Rowan and Claire Reid were in their 20s, hitchhiking around Europe and dropping in on distant relatives. A side trip to Kenya opened Rowan's eyes to an exciting possibility that commercial forestry could be made an attractive option for Australian farming families. Then, in a lucky twist of fate, an unexpected inheritance gave him the opportunity to purchase a property that would enable him to test and demonstrate his beliefs.

> That night, as I fell asleep with the options playing over in my mind ... I dreamt of a treeless valley divided by an eroded creek ... I had a sense that I had dreamt of a real place and, if so, I would find it somewhere close to my childhood home, in the hills of the Otway Ranges. I'd left Australian in search of a future and I found it in a girl that chose to meet my plane in Copenhagen and a dream I had in a cottage in Nairobi. (Reid, 2019, p. 19)

Intrigued by his vivid dream of a treeless valley divided by an eroded creek, Rowan sensed a deeper significance. He felt drawn to the Otway Ranges in western Victoria, near his childhood home. He felt like his dream revealed a real place waiting to be discovered. Upon returning to Australia, Rowan pursued a career as a forestry lecturer while Claire worked as a nurse. In their spare time, they established Bambra Agroforestry Farm on a mostly barren and degraded 42-hectare property.

Over the years, Bambra Agroforestry Farm has transformed into a living laboratory and a symbol of agroforestry principles and practices. More than 10,000 people, including farmers, scientists, conservationists, politicians, policy-makers, students and tree enthusiasts, have visited the farm. They have witnessed first-hand the practical integration of commercial forestry with conventional agriculture. Rowan's expertise has led to the development of undergraduate and postgraduate subjects in agroforestry, as well as the renowned Australian Master TreeGrower Programme (AMTG), which he delivers both domestically and internationally. Recognised as an authority on forestry management practices, Rowan is frequently invited to share his knowledge and experiences in agroforestry. In 2000, he was awarded the prestigious Eureka Museum Prize for Environmental Education, acknowledging his significant contributions through the AMTG.

While Rowan's focus lies on shaping agroforestry's future, Claire supports with family affairs as well as in all aspects of the business. Their property, upon purchase, revealed the stark absence of native trees and vegetation, along with evident waterway erosion and degradation. However, after 35 years of dedicated efforts to implement Rowan's beliefs about incorporating forestry into agricultural land, a remarkable transformation is visible in the improved quality of the land.

This case study serves as a testament to one individual's belief that the false dichotomy between agriculture and forestry can be overcome. This led to the creation of a family business that benefits farmers, foresters and the environment alike. Moreover, it demonstrates the crucial importance of addressing and resolving SDG#15 for current and future generations.

SDG#15 and Bambra Agroforestry Farm

Can cutting down trees save the environment? (Reid, 2019, p. 20)

Bambra Agroforestry Farm envisions a future where nothing separates the descendants of Rowan and Claire from the descendants of the traditional owners of the land, the Gulidjan and Gadubanud peoples. A future characterised by a shared history that all inherit through their connection with, and love for, the country on which they all live and work.

While the UN's SDGs were many decades from being brought into existence, the thinking that motivated Rowan in 1987 was the same as that which underpins SDG#15: how can farms, especially family farms, change their way of operating to reverse the damage caused by traditional western (Anglo-European) farming practices while also remaining viable as productive primary producers?

Rowan defines agroforestry as the integration of trees and shrubs into farming landscapes for conservation and profit. Bambra Agroforestry Farm's mission is to help farmers understand forestry practices that can enhance their farming endeavours, reverse land degradation and mitigate biodiversity loss. Over the past 3 decades, Bambra Agroforestry Farm has worked closely with Australian farmers, promoting selective forestation to improve land productivity. This has helped to create a harmonious balance between environmental, social and economic values.

Rowan's guiding principle is to challenge stereotypes, focus on outcomes and emphasise that it is the motives and knowledge of individuals making land management decisions that truly matter. With this vision and dedication, Bambra Agroforestry Farm has become a beacon of sustainable land management. It showcases the potential for the integration of trees and agriculture to create a prosperous and environmentally conscious future.

By getting farmers to think about trees not only as a means to help rehabilitate and maintain the landscape but also as a commercial crop in their own right, the approach pioneered and demonstrated at Bambra provides a model for the continued operation of independent family farms in a way that is more sustainable and better for the environment while providing additional and alternative income streams for the farmers.

Rowan's mission with Bambra is to teach others the techniques and opportunities for integrating forestry with conventional agriculture. This will conserve the environment, improve biodiversity and reduce and reverse land degradation.

Today the farm grows more than 50 commercial tree species in various planting arrangements and management options. The family business has evolved over time to incorporate a range of products and services in response to customer demands.

To this end, Bambra Agroforestry Farm undertakes three related and overlapping activities indicated in Fig. 3.1:

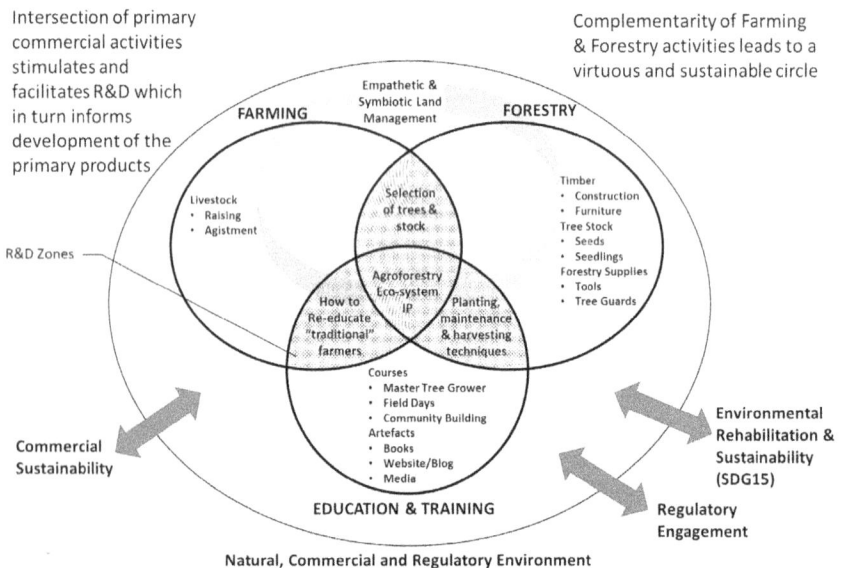

Fig. 3.1.   Related and Overlapping Activities at Bambra. *Source: From Reid (2019).*

(1) Traditional Farming – in this case, raising sheep for wool and/or meat.
(2) Forestry – the propagation, growing and harvesting of trees for high value timber.
(3) Education and Training – training farmers and tree growers in new techniques.

While each of these commonly exist in the agricultural economy as independent businesses, in Bambra's business model these activities overlap, and it is at the intersection of these activities where research and development are undertaken and value (agroforestry intellectual property) is created while the business as a whole serves to demonstrate the benefits of combining two areas of primary production that have traditionally tended to be kept separate.

The intellectual property developed by Rowan through Bambra encompasses:

• Knowledge of and methodologies for selecting the most appropriate trees and stock for a given situation.
• Tree planting, maintenance and harvesting techniques and approaches that maximise the potential for economically viable timber production while repairing and maintaining the local eco-system.
• Methodologies for knowledge transfer to both traditional farmers and tree growers in ways that are relevant to both and provide engagement through shared experience and commonality of purpose.
• A holistic view of the agroforestry environment and enterprise.

Business Model and SDG#15

The primary objective of Bambra Agroforestry Farm is to provide an avenue to transfer this knowledge to farmers and tree growers in an environment that provides a practical demonstration of the specific techniques as well as a living example of the benefits wrought to the landowner, their property and the eco-system as a whole through an integrated approach that is both empathetic and symbiotic to the local environment and eco-system.

Bambra's principal focus is on research and development, consulting and education. Thus, it differs from what is expected of a 'steady state' integrated agroforestry farm which focuses principally on farming or forestry activities. It is crucial to Bambra's mission that the successful integration of farming and forestry activities and the benefits that flow from that integration can be demonstrated and shared. Accordingly, revenue streams from agroforestry activities are secondary in the particular case of Bambra Agroforestry Farm.

By planting trees with a view to land rehabilitation but future harvesting as a high value cash crop, the model pioneered at Bambra provides a direct linkage to SDG#15. Actively managing trees as a crop, then harvesting them for high value uses (timber for construction and furniture making rather than firewood or wood-pulp) ensures that carbon captured during trees' growth and maturation remains sequestered for many decades or even centuries hence.

Using the components of the business model canvas, Bambra's business model demonstrates how environmentally sound practices can make positive business sense (Osterwalder & Pigneur, 2010).

Value Proposition

At the heart of Bambra Agroforestry Farm's business model is a strong value proposition. Mission drives the business not revenue. The mission focuses on effectively communicating about the integration of commercial tree growing and conventional agriculture. Their ultimate goal is to change the rural landscape, making it more diverse, resilient and environmentally sustainable. By promoting agroforestry practices, Bambra offers landholders a model for enhancing land productivity while simultaneously improving environmental outcomes.

The value proposition is summarised as:

- Offering sustainable land management solutions that promote biodiversity conservation.
- Providing education, consultancy and resources to help farmers and landholders implement agroforestry practices and improve productivity sustainably.
- Delivering high-quality agroforestry products that meet market demand and contribute to a more sustainable agricultural sector.

Key Activities

Bambra Agroforestry Farm engages in a range of key activities to fulfil its value proposition and deliver its products and services effectively. These activities include:

- Agroforestry education and consultancy services, providing guidance and knowledge sharing to farmers and landholders interested in adopting sustainable land management practices.
- Tree planting and maintenance, including the integration of native vegetation into farming systems to promote biodiversity and ecosystem health.
- Production and sale of agroforestry products, such as timber, and other sustainable agricultural yields and products.

Key Resources

Several key resources enable Bambra to deliver its value proposition and carry out its key activities. These include:

- Land and natural resources, including the farm's area for agroforestry practices and access to diverse native vegetation.
- Knowledge and expertise in agroforestry techniques, sustainable land management and environmental conservation.
- Strong network of partnerships with stakeholders in the agriculture and environmental sectors.

Customer Segments

Customer segments comprise landholders and individuals interested in sustainable land management practices. These customers can be further segmented based on their specific needs and experience, including:

- Farmers and landholders seeking to adopt sustainable land management practices and improve environmental outcomes.
- Environmental organisations, government agencies and research institutions interested in collaborating on conservation and sustainable agriculture projects.
- Consumers and businesses looking for responsibly sourced agroforestry products.

Channels

To reach its customer segments and deliver its products and services effectively, Bambra Agroforestry Farm utilises a range of channels, both online and offline:

- Direct sales channels, including on-site farm sales, farmers' markets and online platforms, to reach customers and market agroforestry products.
- Workshops, seminars and educational events to disseminate knowledge and attract customers interested in sustainable land management practices.

Customer Relationships

The farm strives to establish relationships characterised by trust, collaboration and ongoing support. Key elements of their customer relationship strategy include:

- Personalised engagement with its customers to give tailored advice, guidance and solutions that address their unique circumstances.
- Knowledge sharing and support through educational programs, publications and online resources ensure customers can seek guidance and address any challenges they encounter.
- Collaboration and networking to actively foster collaboration and networking opportunities among its customers to build a community of like-minded individuals committed to sustainable land management.

Key Partnerships

Bambra Agroforestry Farm recognises the importance of partnerships in achieving its mission and expanding its impact. Key partnership categories include

- Strategic partnerships with local environmental organisations, government agencies and research institutions to collaborate on sustainable land management practices and conservation efforts. Rowan is a founder of the local Landcare group (the Otway Agroforestry Network) and the Australian Agroforestry Foundation.
- Partnerships with suppliers of agroforestry resources and tools to support the farm's operations and provide necessary materials.

Cost Structure

Bambra Agroforestry Farm's cost structure encompasses various elements, including:

- Operational costs, including land maintenance, tree planting, labour and ongoing agroforestry management.
- Research and development expenses for continuous improvement and innovation in sustainable land management practices and product development.
- Marketing and outreach costs to raise awareness about the farm's offerings and attract customers.

Revenue Streams

Bambra generates revenue through multiple streams, including:

- From the sale of agroforestry products, such as timber, fruits and other sustainable agricultural yields and products.
- Education and consultancy services, providing guidance and support to farmers and landholders in implementing agroforestry practices.

The Relationship to SDG#15

Rowan acknowledges the negative impact of family farming on terrestrial ecosystems and believes addressing this issue is crucial. At Bambra, Rowan highlights the need to tackle the root causes of degradation. He focuses on decision-making processes, education, research and landholder support. By supporting family farmers and promoting sustainable practices, Bambra Agroforestry Farm contributes to SDG#15 because it aims to protect, restore and promote terrestrial ecosystem sustainability.

Bambra Agroforestry Farm's impact on SDG#15 is significant.

- Through the integration of trees into farming systems, the farm actively contributes to ecosystem restoration and sustainable land management.
- By enhancing biodiversity, improving soil health and mitigating land degradation, Bambra helps restore and maintain terrestrial ecosystems.
- Bambra's commitment to education and knowledge sharing plays a crucial role in empowering farmers and landholders to adopt sustainable practices.
- Through advocacy efforts and collaboration with stakeholders, Bambra raises awareness about terrestrial ecosystems.
- The positive environmental outcomes resulting from Bambra's agroforestry approach, such as increased carbon sequestration, improved water quality and enhanced wildlife habitat, demonstrate the farm's tangible contributions to SDG#15.
- By continually evaluating its efforts and engaging stakeholders, Bambra makes a positive impact on terrestrial ecosystems and contributes to a sustainable future and measures impact to track progress, ensure accountability and effectively communicate its role in achieving its mission.

Bambra Agroforestry Farm serves as a model for how SDG#15 principles can be translated into real-world action. Although Bambra predates SDG#15, through their commitment to sustainable land management, education and support for family farmers, Bambra demonstrates a lived experience that impacts the protection, restoration and sustainable use of terrestrial ecosystems sought by SDG#15. In so doing, the farm makes a positive impact on terrestrial ecosystems and contributes to a more ecologically friendly future.

Fig. 3.2 illustrates the success of Rowan's forestry and agricultural practices applied to the land at Bambra, providing the evidence for how to make a difference to the environment which Rowan communicates through his community building and consultancy work.

Fig. 3.2.   Bambra – Before and After the Application of Rowan's Agroforestry Principles. *Source:* Used with permission R. Reid (2023).

Challenges Faced by Bambra Agroforestry Farm

The farm faces various challenges in sustainable land management. Bushfire risk is a constant concern, as the farm is situated in a known fire-prone area. This risk, which is not solely attributed to climate change but is exacerbated by it, is a concern for the farm as there is a perceived likelihood that the situation could worsen over time. Bambra Agroforestry Farm also faces a significant challenge related to 'key person' risk due to heavy reliance on Rowan's efforts. As the key figure in the farm's operations, Rowan's role is crucial to Bambra's success and the implementation and dissemination of innovative practices.

However, Rowan identifies another key risk often overlooked – government policies can discourage sustainable practices. For instance, blanket policies prohibiting the harvesting of mature trees, even when they were intentionally planted as a cash crop, create uncertainty and deter farmers from pursuing agroforestry initiatives. The lack of clarity in regulations and potential limitations on tree removal create confusion, hindering farmers' ability to make informed land management decisions.

> I've had to confront local government and say, 'You're going to have to write down on paper exactly what I'm allowed to do ... all your rules are so messy that if I read them one way I'm not allowed to cut a tree down that I planted'.... what does that say to my landholders next door? 'Don't plant trees because they'll stop you cutting them down if there's a koala in them or if they're native'....
> (R. Reid, personal communication, January 18, 2023)

Rowan's frustration with the government's rules and regulations reflects farmers' challenges in navigating these restrictions. This results in loss of agency and non-integrated solutions. This issue, known as 'sovereign risk', hinders community engagement and hampers the progress in achieving sustainability goals.

On the one hand, there is recognition of the importance of sustainable land management and SDG#15 goals. However, government policies are promulgated that serve to discourage the very practices that would contribute to these goals. Blanket policies and unclear regulations create uncertainty and hinder farmers' agroforestry initiatives. This paradoxical situation underscores the need for policy alignment, where regulations support and enable sustainable land management practices rather than impeding them. By addressing this paradox, governments can foster an environment where farmers are empowered to integrate forestry into their farming operations. This will promote the sustainable use of terrestrial ecosystems as envisioned in SDG#15.

Future Plans

Looking ahead, Bambra Agroforestry Farm continues with plans and aspirations for the future. The Reid's immediate focus is on completing the construction of a house using the timber they planted. This endeavour serves as a significant learning experience, enabling the Reid's to confidently sell graded engineering timbers. Rowan also intends to write another book, documenting the house-building process and sharing knowledge from this experience. The farm will continue running educational tours, hosting field days and offering training courses to empower farmers with knowledge and skills. While Rowan's international work has become less of a priority, Bambra Agroforestry Farm continues to make a significant impact within Australia, helping others foster sustainable land management practices and transform agricultural landscapes.

Conclusion

Confront the stereotypes, focus on the outcomes and demonstrate that when it comes to managing our rural landscapes it is not the methods or the tools that are important, but the motives and knowledge of the person making the decisions. (Reid, 2019, p. 20)

Bambra Agroforestry Farm stands as a remarkable example of how the commitment of one person to innovation and sustainable practices can transform the agricultural landscape. It is a living example of the intention of SDG#15. Rowan's vision of integrating trees into farming systems has not only revitalised their own family farm business but also inspired countless farmers and landholders across Australia to embrace agroforestry as a viable and sustainable path forward in addressing the urgent need to protect terrestrial ecosystems.

As Bambra Agroforestry Farm continues to evolve and expand its impact, its dedication to sustainable land management, knowledge sharing and the pursuit of environmental and economic balance serves as an inspiration for the broader agricultural community. By embracing the transformative potential of agroforestry, farmers and landholders can create a more resilient, productive and sustainable future for agriculture in Australia and beyond. This actively contributes to the global efforts needed to achieve SDG#15.

References

Braithwaite, L. W. (1996). Conservation of arboreal herbivores: The Australian scene. *Australian Journal of Ecology, 21*(1), 21–30. https://doi.org/10.1111/j.1442-9993.1996.tb00582.x

Bush Heritage Australia. (2023). Land clearing. *Bush Heritage Australia.* https://www.bushheritage.org.au/what-we-do/our-challenge/land-clearing#anchor

Evans, M. (2016). Deforestation in Australia: Drivers, trends and policy responses. *Pacific Conservation Biology, 22.* https://doi.org/10.1071/PC15052

Mitchell, T. (1838). *Three expeditions into the interior of Eastern Australia, Vol 1 (of 2).* Project Gutenberg.

National Museum of Australia. (2022). Soldier settlement. Defining Moments. *National Museum of Australia.* https://www.nma.gov.au/defining-moments/resources/soldier-settlement#

Osterwalder, A., & Pigneur, Y. (2010). *Business model generation.* John Wiley & Sons.

Reid, R. (2019). *Heartwood: The art and science of growing trees for conservation and profit* (2nd ed.). Melbourne Books.

Reid, R. (2023). Agroforestry in Australia. *Agroforestry.* https://www.agroforestry.net.au/main.asp?_=Home

United Nations. (n.d.). *SDG#15: Promoting the sustainability of terrestrial ecosystems and halting desertification, land degradation, and biodiversity loss.* United Nations. https://sdgs.un.org/goals/goal15

Williams, K., Hunter, B., Schmidt, B., Woodward, E., & Cresswell, D. (2021). Land. *Australia, State of the Environment 2021.* https://soe.dcceew.gov.au/land/introduction

Chapter 4

Australia: Regenerative Agriculture on Echo Hills

Amber Marshall[a], Nikki Thompson[b] and Peter Thompson[b]

[a]Griffith University, Australia
[b]Echo Hills, Australia

Introduction

Echo Hills is a family owned and operated business situated in the Maranoa region in South Western Queensland, Australia. Echo Hills has been in the Thompson family for 75 years as a cropping and cattle operation. Having acquired neighbouring Nugget Hills in 2013, the entire property now spans 80 kms^2. The landscape is characterised by a combination of original forest, substantial creeks, shrubby regrowth and rocky outcrops. The country ranges from rolling open paddocks of Buffel Grass to wild rocky gorges with permanent spring-fed waterholes (see Fig. 4.1).

Summers are generally hot, starting in late October and going through until early March with bursts of 45-degrees celsius maximums in January. Most of the annual 650 mm rainfall occurs in this period. The land responds quickly to rain and can be as rich green as Ireland. However, when the dry season comes, colours of straw-yellow and stark grey are interspersed with grey-green hues of the native timbers. Winter days are generally clear and dry, while nights are cold often getting down below zero degrees Celsius overnight in the June–August period. Spring and autumn are generally quite short and somewhat indistinct.

Peter and Nikki Thompson are the custodians of Echo Hills. Peter Thompson grew up on the farm with his two brothers, taking over operation from his parents, John and Nan Thompson, between 1984 and 1990. Peter and Nikki raised their family of three children Jamie, Ingrid and Andrew at Echo Hills and love to welcome them home with their own children. Emma and Angus King joined the team in 2021 to help manage and steward the cattle and land; they too are raising their three primary school-aged children at Echo Hills.

The Echo Hills team consider themselves an extended family of like-minded and dedicated people seeking new and innovative ways of living in connection with the land and country. The team is passionate about agriculture and its valuable contribution to modern society. The team's diverse expertise covers

Attaining the 2030 Sustainable Development Goal of Life on Land, 41–53
Copyright © 2025 Amber Marshall, Nikki Thompson and Peter Thompson
Published under exclusive licence by Emerald Publishing Limited
doi:10.1108/978-1-83608-212-520241004

Fig. 4.1.   The View Over Echo Hills From the Main Farmhouse.
Source: Peter Thompson.

animals, soil, ecosystems and technology, with a focus on well-being and sustainability of all living things, from humans to microbes!

This chapter tells a story of Life on Land at Echo Hills, with a focus on regenerative agriculture. We describe the bold philosophy, innovative approaches and thoughtful practices of the Echo Hills family farm, which contribute to creating a life on the land that is sustainable, ethical and helps ensure the future of the property beyond the life of its current owners.

Products and/or Services Offered by the Family Business

Echo Hills is a commercial family-run farm whose owners and workers deeply value the pillars of connection, collaboration and community in their daily interactions. Their regenerative approach to agriculture is based on the natural intelligence which permeates living relationships. The key commercial activities, explored below, sit under the umbrella entity *Soil2Soul* (Soil2Soul, 2024).

- *Grazing*. The grazing businesses includes raising Ultrablack cattle breeders, finished grass-fed beef and agistment of other cattle on their property. This is complemented by farming of donkeys and sheep (for meat) as part of on-farm self-sufficiency.

- *Technology testing and commercialisation.* Peter Thompson regularly tests emerging digital technologies in partnership with AgTech providers. These include *AgriWebb* farm data collation, *Optiweigh* livestock monitoring, *Farmbot* remote water monitoring and *Cibo Labs* and *DataFarming* satellite imaging technologies to name a few. Peter also invents, develops and builds farming machines. In 2002, Peter patented a planting point technology (PeterpoinT), with the patent having expired in 2023. This technology is sold nationally through AgPoint on a royalty basis.
- *Consulting.* Nikki Thompson works more in the human ecosystem as a coach and facilitator, working with individuals and small businesses. She has a passion for helping unlock the full and emerging potential that arises when people can bring their full selves into personal and professional relationships. The Thompsons have plans to expand into regenerative agriculture consulting in the future (which they currently do informally).

The Thompsons also participate in coal seam gas (CSG) projects by way of 40 CSG wells and the associated infrastructure of flowlines, pipelines and water transfer stations on their two properties: Echo Hills and Nugget Hills. The Thompsons were one of the first non-gas company owned properties to host operational CSG developments. Peter and Nikki took the view that they were best suited to guide the interface of this new industry with agriculture, with their long history of stewarding the land. Given this, they worked long and hard with Origin Energy to create a transparent, viable and workable agreement that has become the foundation model for CSG industry agreements. Their key criteria were that the land came first, followed closely by agriculture, with their personal liveability having critical importance. They view the money coming from CSG as compensation, not income, for their role in protecting the land.

Vision and Mission

The Echo Hills vision is *Healthy food, healthy soil and a healthy place to live*. This vision is underpinned by the notion that soil, plants and animals work in collaboration to produce nutritious food and regenerate the land and life. Nature has billions of years of experience in the symbiotic creation of life and the Thompsons, as stewards, are here to listen, learn and respond.

To achieve this vision, the Echo Hills team aspires to be leaders in regenerative agriculture. While there is no accepted definition of regenerative agriculture, one that resonates with the Thompsons is as follows.

> As a philosophy and approach to land management, regenerative agriculture asks us to think about how all aspects of agriculture are connected through a web – a network of entities who grow, enhance, exchange, distribute, and consume goods and services – instead of a linear supply chain. (Natural Resources Defence Council (NRDC), 2024, para. 3)

A crucial association between the Echo Hills vision and this conception of regenerative agriculture is that all things that live on land – plants, animals and people – are connected by the soil. This is reflected in the *Soil2Soul* name given to the parent entity of the Echo Hills family business. This approach also resonates with the following more scientific definition of regenerative farming.

> An approach to farming that uses soil conservation as the entry point to regenerate and contribute to multiple provisioning, regulating and supporting ecosystem services, with the objective that this will enhance not only the environmental, but also the social and economic dimensions of sustainable food production. (Schreefel et al., 2020, p. 5)

The Echo Hills team's approach to realising their vision through regenerative farming is underpinned by guiding values and principles that inform everything they do. The following summaries the principles and values for regenerative agriculture at Echo Hills farm.

Principles that guide what they do
Experiential practical knowledge, invention and innovation,
Acknowledging and working with natural intelligence,
Embracing technology and emerging innovation as part of how they function and
Looking at new ways of living in connection with country/land.

Values that guide how they work
Relationship-based business – local, national and global,
Non-hierarchical relationship with the land, sharing resources and knowledge
Syntropic practices – handing things back in better condition than they were found and
(Bio)diversity of land and people.

Background to the Family and the Business

John Thompson's Legacy

While the Thompson family have been custodians of the land at Echo Hills for 75 years, they acknowledge that the land was stewarded by the Yiman people for thousands of years prior to that. As Indigenous stories acknowledge, humans have evolved from the Earth, as have the Thompson family living and working on the land over the decades.

Arriving in a Willy's Jeep meandering through dense scrub in 1949, Peter's father, John, came to Echo Hills believing this country to be 'good sheep country.' It was back-breaking work in the early days with minimal mechanical assistance and little infrastructure. Land was cleared to allow the running of livestock with cattle soon taking over from sheep. Farming cereal crops was introduced to help manage the brigalow regrowth. It is essential to understand the ethos of the times, as this story is told. In those early years, there was governmental pressure to develop the country to feed the nation and grow the economy. The passions of the individual custodians intermingled with the possibilities that the environmental and political context allowed.

Being raised with the instructions from John Thompson to always 'keep your eyes open', great observational skills were honed in the family. Peter, as middle of three sons, always had an innate love of the land. As a young adult working with his father, at times they 'butted horns' around whether grain or cattle should have 'right of way', each having their justification.

Peter also inherited a keen interest in technology from his father, who was a champion of invention and innovation. In the 1960s and 1970s, John Thompson spearheaded the local progress association and was at the forefront of developing better ways to do things, on farm and in the community. Like his father, Peter is concerned with finding simple solutions to actual problems.

Changing With the Times

At Echo Hills, technological changes have walked hand-in-hand with a growing commitment to regenerative agriculture over the decades. Starting with a 1923 Fordson tractor, mechanical support for farm work has increased in size, complexity and efficiency. And, like all technologies, this has come with pros and cons. A deep philosophical premise held by the Echo Hills team is that technology is a tool that needs to be utilised in service of the vision the team upholds.

Profitability must be taken into account to be responsible land stewards, but the Thompsons see profit as a precessional outcome, i.e. a natural consequence of being good land stewards. Profitability also does not mean that every single aspect of the business will make money; some aspects of the business fund others for overall benefit to land and life. This process is iterative, creating the conditions for growth in all domains, rather than being super-focused on one service or product. Over the years farming practices have involved: shifting cattle from cropping country to ensure compaction is minimised; rotating crops; naturally maintaining soil fertility and redesigning paddock lay out to minimise water runoff and erosion.

As knowledge about sustainable agriculture and technology evolved, changes occurred at Echo Hills. The family has always been curious and motivated to change as new evidence comes to light. However, the Thompsons don't invest in new things just because they are new or to 'keep up with the Joneses.' With his fascination with technology, Peter is an excellent mechanic and handyman. Living on the land and isolated from many services, making do is often a necessity, so there is a strong ethos of reduce, reuse and recycle. How this philosophy and associated practices align with SGD#15 is explored below.

SDG#15: Life on Land and Echo Hills Farm

The Thompsons' commitment to sustainable life on the land began well before establishment of the UN Sustainability Development Goals (SDGs). The seeds for innovative approaches to farming, which prioritised the long-term sustainability of the land over maximising short-term productivity and profits, were planted 75 years ago. Informed by John Thompson's belief one should always hand things back in better condition than when they found them, Peter and Nikki have strived to improve the condition of their land over time while maintaining a commercially viable business. While it has not been their explicit intention to be guided by the SDGs, the Echo Hills team contribute to several of SDG#15's targets. While these practices are inter-twined, they are explored below in relation to each target.

SDG#15.1: Conserve and Restore Terrestrial and Freshwater Ecosystems

Echo Hills is in a region within Queensland which has a 'reliably unreliable rainfall.' Since the Thompson family arrived, they have lived and worked within those parameters. Always having been dry land graziers and farmers, they have spent decades working to conserve precious water. Living on the eastern fall of the Great Dividing Range, their water run-off is subject to responsibility and regulation related to protecting the Great Barrier Reef. The freshwater courses, namely Slate Hill and Eurombah Creeks, running through the property flow into the Dawson River, Fitzroy River and eventually run into the Reef at Rockhampton some 400 kms away. The Echo Hills team protects both Slate Hill and Eurombah Creeks from runoff through fencing, ensuring waterways are grassed, and undertaking structured management of livestock in those areas. The goal is to ensure, as much as possible, that clear water is entering the off stream.

Water supply to the property is sourced from one deep-flowing Artesian bore and four sub-Artesian bores. All the water used on the property is for domestic and stock use, with free-to-air water supplies limited to closed poly tanks, which minimises water loss through evaporation. These bores are interlinked which provides redundancy and flexibility of supply. The Thompsons also follow water management principles established by Peter's great grandfather; that is, manage the land to ensure effective management of overground water to supplement the bore water. Tank water is also used for the houses on the property.

SDG#15.3: End Desertification and Restore Degraded Land

In 2020, the Thompsons made a bold decision to cease continual cropping, which previously included wheat, oats, barley, chickpeas, sorghum and mung beans. Cropping had been the farm's primary income stream for over 40 years, in line with many others in the region. The decision was prompted by a more ambitious focus on regenerative farming. Specifically, they replaced continual cropping with managed grazing.

Managed grazing involves fluctuating the cattle stock in paddocks depending on land conditions. This allows the Echo Hills team to balance original and transitional biodiversity; that is, encourage regrowth of traditional trees and shrubs while maintaining enough non-native Buffel grass and other introduced species such as Chicory and Desmanthus to feed cattle. The Thompsons achieve variable stock rates by charging other people a fee to agist their animals. When land condition is good, more animals are brought in; when land condition is poor, stocks are lowered to allow the land to recover.

The Thompsons' approach to managed grazing is driven by their commitment to soil health as the foundation of regenerative agriculture, which is further aligned with SDG#15.3. As Peter says, 'It's not the cow, it's the how'; this means that looking after the land means the cow will also be looked after in the process of regenerative farming.

In contrast to the accepted norm of blade ploughing or treating with granular herbicide to eradicate regrowth, the Thompsons aim to keep a healthy balance of trees shrubs and grass. Their method is to run a light pulling chain over the regrowth every 5–7 years seasons, depending on conditions. This breaks off the shrubbery and low trees to form a rich mulch on the ground. The plants aren't killed in this process; rather they are activated to grow. It is like a largescale pruning or 'chop and drop' technique, a syntropic farming principle.

Significant strips and clumps of mature trees are left or added over the years, resulting in a landscape that has a wide diversity of plants and growth stages, all the while providing essential ground cover. Independent soil testing by the state government Department of Primary Industries, as well as farm records, show this style of management has increased soil carbon levels up to 25% higher than virgin scrub. The Thompsons have numerous photos showing severely degraded and eroding areas completely rehabilitated within 3–5 years.

At the same time, careful management of livestock and judicious culling of excess macropods returns the land to a healthy balance. The Thompsons note that achieving land restoration is complex and can impact other SDGs; and there is a need to balance traditional and transitional biodiversity. Peter says, 'To most people, according to the criteria, two Caterpillar tractors with a scrub pulling chain between them, is deforesting. And yet we're increasing the soil carbon and keeping the water cleaner.'

SDG#15.5: Protect Biodiversity and Natural Habitats

While the focus for the original Echo Hills cropping paddocks is restoration, the Nugget Hills part of the property offers opportunities for maintenance of 6,000 acres of native bushland. This area is managed through controlled burning. Cool and hot burning techniques help manage and keep understory fuel levels under control, and fire breaks and access tracks help manage seasonal fire outbreaks. At times, light grazing is used in these 'native' areas to keep grass down and prevent catastrophic fire. Mechanical interventions are also used from time to time, such as 'ripping' using a chisel plough to aerate hard pans created by humans or livestock.

By keeping the water and land as healthy as possible, parts of Echo Hills and Nugget Hills are excellent habitat for native animals, birds, fish and other animals, which contributes directly to SDG#15.5. Several species that are found on the property including: birds (e.g. Jabiru, wedgetail eagles, sea eagles, pelicans, wrens and wood ducks); water animals (e.g. freshwater fish, platypus, mussels and turtles); mammals/marsupials (e.g. dingo, koala, echidna, wallaroo, gliders, wallabies) and reptiles (e.g. green frogs, goannas, pythons and other snakes). The Thompsons also collaborate with other organisations to conduct research into the animal life on their properties. For example, they have worked with *Boobook Explore*, an ecological tour company based in Roma, to investigate the white throated turtle that inhabits Eurombah Creek.

It is important to note that some native animals in remote Australia have become so populous that they have become a pest due to overgrazing and land degradation. When the Thompsons first took over Nugget Hills, they needed to significantly cull wallabies and kangaroos as they were decimating the land, especially in cropping paddocks which they had turned into dust bowls.

Accordingly, the Thompsons take a balanced approach to biodiversity. Recognising that their property is both a place for restoration and commercial operation, they strive to create biodiversity that is fit-for-purpose rather than attempt to restore the land to its absolute original condition. Peter said, 'Echo Hills is known to have significant biodiversity, but not all necessarily original – this is a good thing as it means overall greater diversity.'

Beyond the Business: Connection, Collaboration and Community

The team at Echo Hills aims to extend their impact into the broader community through various advocacy and volunteer activities that augment the overall vision and mission. These activities fall into the broad categories of connection, collaboration and community. Though they overlap in various ways, we provide some distinct examples below and link them with SDG#15, specifically *SDG#15.9: Integrate ecosystems and biodiversity values into national and local planning*.

Connection

The Thompsons work hard to remain connected to their staff internally and to other stakeholders externally, which is achieved through their organisational structure. Hierarchy does play a role in the structure at Echo Hills, but it is a natural hierarchy rather than one built on job titles. Each member of the team has a unique and emergent skillset and passions and that is respected as decision-making opportunities arise. While planning is a vital part of this, intuition is also highly valued as part of the process. The arrival of Angus, Emma and their family to Echo Hills in 2021 is an example of that. A short job description sent to several people who 'felt right', followed up by personal communication and honest conversations, saw Nikki and Peter attract and retain the 'right' people for the job. Unknown connections and synchronicities emerge from this type of embodied, values-driven growth.

These connections, informed by frequent, open and clean communication, extends beyond the farm to the community, local and further afield. While the Echo Hills team is aiming to create a microcosm that is generative, knowing the ripple effect that will have, they also work strategically to create connections that are based on trust and mutual respect in the wider community. From involvements in national committees to having a broad network of colleagues globally (including some from working at Echo Hills as backpackers). In support of SDG#15.9 and its focus on influencing governance systems external to the farm, Echo Hills' web of connectivity is vital for creating a field of trust so that stories can be shared to create a greater awareness and understanding of the role of primary producers and land custodians in our modern and increasingly urbanised world.

Collaboration

The Thompsons have always been involved in community organisations and advocacy. Nikki's passions have been more in the arena of education and health whilst Peter's have had an agricultural focus. Peter is currently Chair of the National Farmers' Federation (NFF) sub-committee on Telecommunications and Social Policy. He is also on the NFF working group for the Farm Data Code, the CSG taskforce and previously the NFF Workplace Relations committee. Nikki is on an advisory committee for Australian College of Rural and Remote Medicine (ACRRM). Both Peter and Nikki are members of the Macintyre Alliance, not-for-profit organisation that brings together like-minded farmers in western Queensland with an interest in how to improve the way they manage their farms and natural assets. They are also involved in organisations looking at regenerative ways of doing business including Syntropic World (Syntropic World, 2024), New Economy Network Australia (NENA, 2024), Australian Earth Laws Alliance (AELA, 2024) and the global Warm Data Lab (Warm Data Lab, 2024) community.

In their work to promote healthy rural communities, the Thompsons are active members of Remote Australians Matter, a local organisation seeking to advance a new community-driven, place-based models of primary healthcare that are innovative, equitable, appropriate, well-funded and sustainable for remote Australia. Nikki Thompson also writes a weekly column for their local paper *Maranoa Today*. These are inspiring stories of local residents who all play a part in creating vibrant and healthy communities.

The Thompsons' thought leadership and consistent engagement with diverse audiences directly and indirectly contributes to SDG#15.9 in helping to integrate ecosystems and biodiversity values into national and local planning.

Community

As noted above, the impact of Echo Hills farm's SDG-aligned vision, mission and values are felt at the local, national and even international levels. The Thompsons are known for doing things a little bit differently. Other farmers who have 'looked over the fence' at Echo Hills have begun to question how they do business. Peter and Nikki are always open to answering questions but are mindful of not trying to 'convert' others to their way of thinking. Nikki says that leading by example in regenerative farming 'slowly gives people permission to look more deeply at what may be possible and feel comfortable to have a go and see for themselves.'

Echo Hills has attracted both praise and criticism from industry and the media. The Thompsons have been widely praised for spearheading regenerative agriculture in the cropping sector. For example, in 1998, Peter and Nikki won National Grain Growers of the Year Award for their prime hard wheat. The award was not simply based on yield, but criteria included land health, grain quality, record keeping showing data-supported decision-making and local business and community support.

Finally, both Peter and Nikki are regularly called upon experts to make comments in the media about agriculture, sustainability, rural development and technology. For example, in 2023, alongside other national experts, they were guests on a three-part series on digital regenerative agriculture on the *Digital Village* podcast (Digital Village, 2023). The Thompsons have also shared their wisdom at national and international conferences, further contributing to SDG#15.9.

The Role of Technology in Achieving SDG#15

Collectively, the Echo Hills team has moved from generalist to specialist over the decades, and now that pendulum is moving towards an integration of those parts. Technology can play a huge part in that integration process as computing power can assist the human journey. The Thompsons are deeply in favour of hybrid models (digital-human) as they move towards being truly generative. Peter cautions using digital technologies for its own sake and insists that 'technology should enhance our people, not replace them'.

Peter Thompson is an early adopter and national thought leader in digital technology adoption for regenerative agriculture (see Fig. 4.2). Even before digital technology was commonplace on farms, Peter was using tramline farming in the 1980s to reduce soil compaction and overlap in cropping situations, which reduced inputs such as fuel, seed, fertiliser and herbicide, and helps to achieve SDG#15.1 to conserve and restore terrestrial and freshwater ecosystems. Tractors moved to being GPS-guided in the early 1990s. With a passion for mapping, Peter integrated high resolution aerial photography with satellite mapping to ensure his 'eyeometer' was farming the potentially erodible slopes in a manner that, in his words 'would keep the paddock in the paddock.'

Not one for convention, Peter developed a farming method that saw him remove costly and highly interventionist contour banks on old cultivations; these banks were also not needed in new developments. He did this by reading the land, then using the longest, straightest planting runs within the natural contour constraints, utilised the natural gullies and watercourses to safely carry excess water ('just as nature had designed them'). This resulted in higher rainfall infiltration leading to higher yields and little-to-no erosion on cropping paddocks. These uses of technology to work with rather than against the land contributes directly to SDG#15.3 to end desertification.

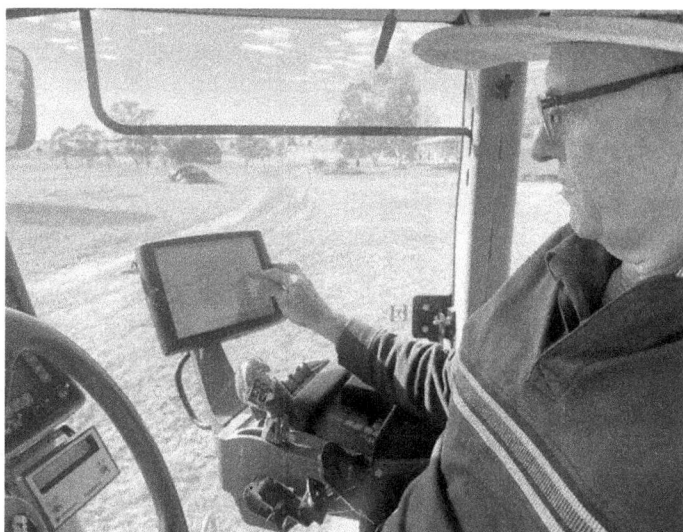

Fig. 4.2.   Peter Thompson Operating GPS and Autosteer on the Quadtrac Tractor. *Source:* Peter Thompson.

Other technologies also enhance the capacity of Echo Hills to contribute to SDG targets by enabling the team to track some of their activities and measure some of the impact they are having on the land through interventions. For example, soil testing, pasture sampling and dung sampling technologies are used to observe trends (i.e. soil carbon or fertility changes over time) and inform land and animal management practices. Farmbot is used for monitoring of water tanks and water consumption by stock. Combined with 'warm data' (e.g. human observation of manure shape, dung beetle activity, insect activity, soil condition and koala scratchings) these datasets help the Thompsons make choices that help conserve and restore water (SDG#15.1), land (SDG#15.3) and habitat (SDG#15.5).

A continuing mantra in Australian agriculture is 'you can't manage what you can't measure', as stated in 2023 by Tony Mahar, then CEO of National Farmers Federation (NFF, 2023). However, Peter and Nikki do not subscribe to this instrumentalist view of farming and land management; it is counter-intuitive to their philosophy of working in collaboration with nature, which cannot be controlled absolutely, though some farming systems may attempt this. Instead, the Thompsons view digital technologies as powerful tools to assist in decision-making but not automate it. This broadly aligns SDG#15 in terms of living on land in harmony with it, rather than seeking to dominate it.

What Next for Echo Hills Farm and SDG#15?

A major change the Thompsons are working towards is a redefinition of land management from ownership to stewardship. Just as Indigenous cultures saw the land as owning them, rather than the other way around, the Echo Hills team is looking at new models that include self-owning land and the concept of tradeable digital twins. This is very 'outside the box' thinking in the current economic reality, but these concepts are gaining traction. In the current economic system that is market driven and externalises nature in general, those working in agriculture are not only producers of food and energy but are also undervalued custodians of natural resources. Future models need to embrace that diversity and realise that there will never be 'black and white, one size fits all' answers to the deep questions that *Nature* poses.

Broadening the concept of family is something else the Thompsons see as an important step forward for the family farm. This includes connecting with like-minded and open-hearted others who share a common passion and bring their unique skills to the table. Honest communication and a willingness to be wrong and to continually learn and grow are critical, replacing old ideas of intergenerational succession or selling the farm as the only options. They say, 'we see our farm as a place to help grow understanding and practical custodian skills. A place to learn and grow self, others, food and our relationships to Earth. A place where the business-as-usual model can be challenged through the lens of how natural systems work rather than dictated by human constructs that externalise and devalue nature.' Fig. 4.3 shows the 'Welcome sign' that the Thompsons have created to welcome those to the land of which they are the current custodians.

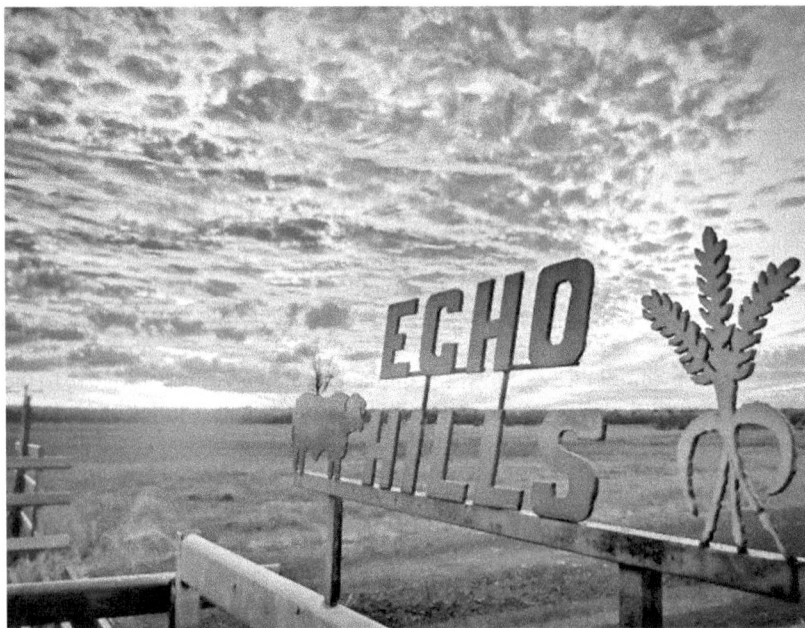

Fig. 4.3.   Welcome Sign Made by Peter Thompson. *Source:* Peter Thompson.

They plan to use the Principles of the Earth Charter (Earth Charter, 2024) as guidelines moving forward.

- Respect the Earth and all its diversity,
- Care for the community of life with understanding, compassion and love,
- Build democratic societies that are just, participatory, sustainable and peaceful and
- Secure Earth's bounty and beauty for present and future generations.

The Thompsons say, 'this feels like a life well lived.'

Acknowledgements

The authors acknowledge the traditional owners of the land where Echo Hills farm is situated, on Yiman country in Queensland. The authors give gratitude to all those who have walked, lived and cared for this land since humans evolved in this place. The authors have been and always will be owned and grown by this land. May we all remember that as we journey forward together collaboratively as true custodians.

References

Australian Earth Laws Alliance. (2024). Who we are. *Australian Earth Laws Alliance.* https://www.earthlaws.org.au/

Digital Village. (2023). Responsible Innovation in AgTech Pt.1. *Digital Village.* https://digitalvillage.network/the-digital-village-podcast/

Earth Charter. (2024). The Earth Charter. *Earth Charter.* https://earthcharter.org/read-the-earth-charter/

National Farmers' Federation. (2023, September 13). World-first research suggests natural capital impacts farm performance. *National Farmers Federation.* https://nff.org.au/media-release/world-first-research-suggests-natural-capital-impacts-farm-performance/

Natural Resources Defence Council (NRDC). (2024). Regenerative agriculture 101. *NRDC.* https://www.nrdc.org/stories/regenerative-agriculture-101

New Economy Network Australia. (2024). New Economy Network Australia. *New Economy Network Australia.* https://www.neweconomy.org.au/

Schreefel, L., Schulte, R., De Boer, I., Schrijver, A., & Van Zanten, H. (2020). Regenerative agriculture–the soil is the base. *Global Food Security*, *26*, 100404. https://doi.org/10.1016/j.gfs.2020.100404

Soil2Soul. (2024). Soil2Soul: Growing food, nourishing people. *Soil2Soul.* https://soil2soul.com.au/

Syntropic World. (2024). Welcome to syntropic word. *Syntropic World.* https://syntropic.world/

Warm Data Lab. (2024). What is warm data? *Warm Data Lab.* https://warmdatalab.net/warm-data

Chapter 5

Honduras: Del Lago Orgánico

Marcio Paz[a], Rebeca Paz[a] and Allan Discua Cruz[b]

[a]Del Lago Orgánico S de RL, Honduras
[b]Lancaster University Management School, UK

Introduction

Del Lago Orgánico S de RL (DLO) is a family business located in Tegucigalpa, department of Francisco Morazán, Honduras, Central America. The company produces single origin, 100% natural products derived from coffee, cacao, green plantain, sweet potato, cassava, taro and others. Within its product line, they also include specialty coffee, coffee pulp and cacao husk infusions, gluten-free flours, cacao powder and sugar-free chocolate. All these products have an international certification granted by The Vegan Society. The company was founded by Marcio Paz and his children Marcio Fernando Paz and Rebeca Paz in 2021. The company is committed to four axes: (i) producing healthy and natural products, (ii) having a line of products within the reach of society, (iii) producing with quality and (iv) protect the environment. Fig. 5.1a shows the current logo and Fig. 5.1b shows the company brand.

Fig. 5.1.   (a) Company Logo and (b) Company Brand.

Attaining the 2030 Sustainable Development Goal of Life on Land, 55–66
Copyright © 2025 Marcio Paz, Rebeca Paz and Allan Discua Cruz
Published under exclusive licence by Emerald Publishing Limited
doi:10.1108/978-1-83608-212-520241005

Del Lago Orgánico y Finca La Fé

DLO is made up of two ventures: A processing plant located in Tegucigalpa, department of Francisco Morazán, capital of Honduras where the raw materials are processed that come from their farm, Finca La Fé. Finca la Fé is located close to Lake Yojoa, the largest lake in Honduras, about 170 km north of Tegucigalpa.

Finca la Fé (Farm The Faith, in Spanish) was named as such in 2015 out of the conviction of starting a dream based on faith in God. This farm began in 1965, producing coffee and cardamom, by René Adalberto Paz Alfaro, father and grandfather of the founders of DLO. In 2015, Marcio Paz decided to leave his professional life and return to Honduras to continue the family legacy in the farm. Upon his return, Marcio restructured the management and growth approach of Finca la Fé. The farm was then reorganised, recovering lost or unattended areas, and diversified into new crops, such as cacao, green plantain and others under an agro-forestry system, prioritising the conservation of existing natural areas and forests.

Products and/or Services Offered by the Family Business

The products Del Lago Orgánico cultivates have a focus on health and nutrition, that is, 100% natural of organic origin and always with the priority of producing with quality, environmentally sustainable and with care for the natural ecosystem that they have or that they can contribute to improving.

DLO organizes its production lines as follows:

- Specialty Coffee and Infusions,
- Gluten-free Flours,
- Cacao Derivatives and
- Sugar-free Chocolate.

The following are products DLO offers:

Coffee and Infusions

Specialty Coffee, Washed Process
Specialty Coffee, Honey Process
Coffee Pulp Infusion
Cocoa Husk Infusion

Gluten Free Flours

Banana Flour (Green Plantain Flour)
Sweet Potato Flour
Cassava Flour
Malanga or Taro Flour
Coffee Pulp Flour
Cocoa Husk Flour
Rice Flour *

Cocoa Derivatives

Cocoa Powder, 100% natural
Cocoa Butter
Roasted Cocoa Nibs

Sugar Free Chocolate

Dark Chocolate Spread, sugar free
Dark Chocolate Spread with Almonds, sugar free
Dark Chocolate Cashew Spread, sugar free
Traditional Hot Chocolate, sugar free
Hot Chocolate with Saffron and Cardamom, sugar free
Hot Chocolate in Almond Mug, sugar free *
Hot Chocolate in Mocha Mug. sugar free *
90%, 80%, 70%, 65%, 60% Sugar Free Chocolate Bars*

All products are vegan certified by The Vegan Society (*in process) since 2022.
In 2024, DLO has started the Kosher certification process.

Vision and Mission

The vision of DLO is to be recognized as a premium and differentiated company in their business sector, with organic, single-origin, artisanal, healthy and nutritious products for their consumers, providing fair treatment to their strategic partners and committed to environmental conservation.

The mission of DLO is to be a transformative company of agricultural products, with unique origins, 100% organic and natural, offering products that provide a satisfying experience for their consumers who seek quality, care for their health and nutrition, valuing environmentally friendly processes and with a socially responsible business model.

The values of DLO are loyalty, responsibility, trust, honesty and fairness.

Background to the Family and the Business

DLO was founded in 2021 by Marcio Paz, Marcio Fernando Paz and Rebeca Paz as Del Lago Orgánico S de RL de CV (DLO). It emerged as an initiative of Marcio Fernando and Rebeca, after hurricanes Eta and Iota devastated almost 75% of the crops at Finca La Fé in November 2020.

The inspiring words of Marcio Fernando and Rebeca were as follows:

> Let's start something that is healthy and nutritious. We can do it Dad! You have the experience and God has always been with us. We can begin with what we have left. (M. Fernando and R. Paz, personal communication, November 1, 2020)

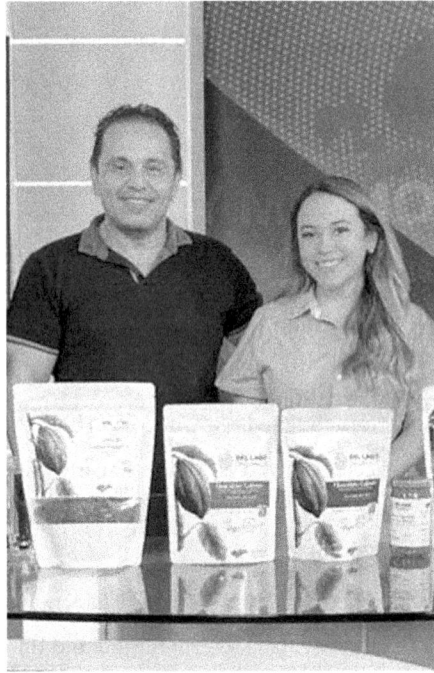

Fig. 5.2.   Marcio (L) and Rebeca (R) Promoting Products From Del Lago Orgánico in a TV Show.

In December 2020, the dream began to take shape. The installation of a processing plant in 2021 in Tegucigalpa was accelerated. Manufacturing processes were certified via international certifications, registrations and permits. The local market began to open in February 2022. Fig. 5.2 shows Marcio and Rebeca Paz promoting DLO products.

As a family in business, the Paz family affirm the importance of taking care of their family legacy on the farm and the ecosystem that God has given them to steward. The forest and care of everything related to its operation is a priority in all their endeavours.

The Paz family have built their DLO projects with the following value premise:

> Our products satisfy the need to consume healthy and nutritious products, promoting health care and at the same time promoting environmental care and awareness. We are Honduran producers from the field to the final product: growing, harvesting, transforming and marketing our own raw materials. Our line of products has an international vegan certificate, guaranteeing a high standard of quality and being 100% organic and natural. (M. Paz, personal communication, June 1, 2024)

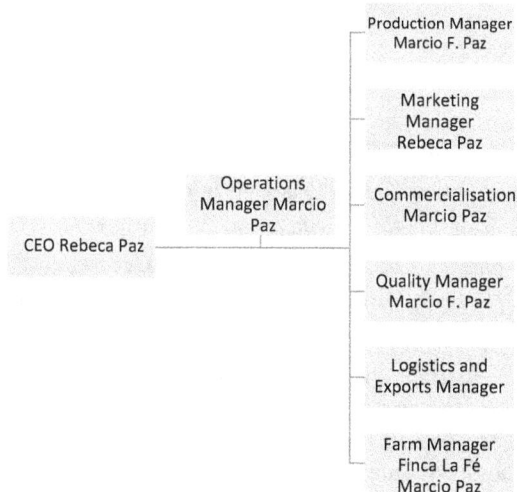

Fig. 5.3.   Organisation Chart of Del Lago Orgánico S de RL.

Rooted in religious convictions, the family acknowledge how God is blessing them with and through their finca. For the family, their faith guides them in committing their projects to protect Finca La Fé whilst manufacturing healthy and nutritional products for their customers.

Currently, their organisation can be visualised in the organisation chart in Fig. 5.3. Their organisation is still evolving, and they hope as a goal to be able to integrate valuable human resources in the coming years.

Table 5.1 provides a summary of some of the most important moments the family business has faced in the past few years.

Table 5.1. Milestones of Finca la Fé and DLO.

Date	Milestone
2015	Marcio Paz *begins evaluation of Finca La Fé* and its operational rearrangement
2016	*Planting* of coffee, cocoa, banana and agroforestry system *begins*
2016	*Marcio Paz completes a Diploma in Organic Agriculture* at COMSA. Marcio initiates operations of organic agriculture and introduces best agricultural practices
2017	The process of *certifying the Finca La Fé forests,* under the PESA plan (special agroforestry sustainability plan) managed by IHCAFE and ICF, is completed
2020	Hurricanes Eta and Iota *destroy 75% of Finca la Fé.* November

(Continued)

Table 5.1. *(Continued)*

Date	Milestone
2021	The Paz family decides to *accelerate the processing plant project* with ideas from Marcio Fernando and Rebeca. January
2021	Del Lago Orgánico S de RL is *legally constituted.* May
2021	The granting of *Vegan Certification.* November
2021	*Packaging and logo design* are completed. December
2022	*The start of operations* in the national market. February
2022	DLO participates in *Feria Bazar del Sabado.* February
2022	*Honourable Mention Award. Sustainable Companies Competition* sponsored by Bosques & Co. Only Central American company who was one of the top 10 finalists. It allows DLO to procure long-term credit line and low interest rate by INDUSTRIAL BANK (Guatemala) as an innovative project. Achieved by Marcio Paz. August
2022	*3rd Place Award. Girl Boss Business and Entrepreneurial Women* sponsored by Revista Estilo and Banco Ficohsa. Capital seed and Advertising Award. Achieved by Rebeca Paz. September 2022
2023	*2nd Place Award. Comprehensive Business Model Competition* sponsored by Terra Te Impulsa of the Terra Group and the Tegucigalpa Chamber of Commerce. Seed capital. Achieved by Marcio Paz. June
2023	Rebeca Paz becomes member of Voces Vitales. June
2023	*1st Place Award.* Winner of the BAC *Business Award for Young Women Entrepreneurs. Triple Impact Sustainability Project.* Seed capital. Achieved by Rebeca Paz. August
2023	*First Production Line Expansion.* September
2023	Reached *HNL 1,000,000 in sales.* September
2023	3rd place Award. *Premio Road to Innovate. Central American Regional Event* in Guatemala, sponsored by Friedrich Naumann Stiftung INNOVATE Entrepreneurship Programme 2024. Participation Marcio Fernando Paz. November
2023	Agreement to commit to SDGs as organizational policy. November
2023	Invitation by the Secretary of Economic Development (SDE) to participate as an *Exhibiting Company in the Shanghai Fair, China.* Selected as 1 of 20 exhibiting companies nationwide. Rebeca Paz participated. November
2024	*Financing Line* granted by Bosques & Co. A financing line of $15,000 to invest in the expansion of the company's production capacity. January

Table 5.1. *(Continued)*

Date	Milestone
2024	*Second production line expand.* April-June
2024	Selected as one of six companies to participate as a *representative of Honduras at the LAC FLAVOR 2024 Fair in Manaus, Brazil.* Nomination and selection by the IDB (Inter-American Development Bank) and the SDE. Marcio Paz participation. June

SDG#15: Life on Land and Del Lago Orgánico S de RL de CV

SDG#15, Life on Land, has as its main objective 'Protect, restore and promote sustainable use of terrestrial ecosystems, sustainably manage forests, combat desertification, and halt and reverse land degradation and halt biodiversity loss' (United Nations, n.d.). When shaping DLO's vision and mission, the family gave relevance to SDG#15 through their actions to conserve the ecosystem within the farm and its surroundings.

Finca La Fé is located near Lake Yojoa, the only natural lake in the country, a region known for its abundant biodiversity in terms of flora and fauna. Such setting generates the awareness of safeguarding the natural environment surrounding the lake, contributing to conserve a freshwater ecosystem (SDG#15.1). The farm is surrounded by livestock farms, where deforestation has been evident and widespread. By preserving the natural ecosystem, the farm has become a small lung in the area. In the process of organising the farm, the natural wealth is visualised through a rich diversity of trees, plants, birds and terrestrial animals. Such context has heightened in the family the need to conserve and protect life on land.

In 2016, support was requested from the Honduran Coffee Institute (IHCAFE) and the Forest Conservation Institute (ICF) to be the recipient of a certification known as the Special Agroforestry Sustainability Plan (PESA). It was then possible to determine that Finca La Fé has a natural wealth of more than 40 species of trees, between 45 and 50 species of birds and more than 30 species of land animals. Unfortunately, the PESA project was short-lived, and certification was not achieved. However, a family decision was made to declare 15 hectares of forest as a protected nature reserve area. The goal would be to safeguard this area to protect the natural environment, aligning our vision with SDG#15.4 (ensure the conservation of mountain ecosystems, including their biodiversity) and SDG#15.5 (protect biodiversity and its natural habitat). For DLO, it is a priority to preserve and encourage protective agriculture practices, including zero deforestation, zero agrochemicals, zero burning and zero herbicides and pesticides.

Since there are no official organisation in Honduras that grant a certification of protected areas, the Paz family decided to look after their natural environment and establish a series of objectives, including zero deforestation and protection of the natural ecosystem (UNECE, n.d.), which is fully in line with the targets and indicators of SDG#15.

DLO was born with a strong ethos around organic agriculture. DLO produces its own biofertilizers. The Paz family completed training by the Cooperativa Orgánica Marcala S.A (COMSA) and received a Diploma in Organic Agriculture and immediately implemented their learning into their processes. Supported by religious beliefs, the family commitment was imprinted from the beginning by understanding the importance of what God gave them to steward and doing a small part for humanity.

From the beginning the Paz family sought support from governmental institutions with little success as no support or guidance was provided. However, this did not stop them and out of their personal conviction and resources family members bricolage their approach. The idea of continuously seeking certifications was spearheaded by Marcio Paz who transmitted that feeling to his children, who have supported the idea wholeheartedly.

> We understand that there is a lot to do but we try to communicate the issue of conservation on our networks or in any program, forum, or event where we are invited. Our staff takes care of the environment, the forest, the animals. They no longer burn cultivated areas [traditional method in the region] and we have tried to instil healthy agricultural practices. (M. Paz, personal communication, June 1, 2024)

This approach has allowed DLO to integrate SDG#15.1 (conservation, restoration and sustainable use of terrestrial land) and SDG#15.4 (ensure the conservation of mountain ecosystems, including their biodiversity) and SDG#15.5 (protect biodiversity and natural habits).

DLO is currently trying to get involved with the REHNAP (Honduran Network of Private Natural Reserves), an institution that has gradually achieved notoriety in the country. Through REHNAP, DLO plans to bring forward professional training and association with people who wish to preserve their heritage and establish themselves as a Natural Reserve for the country, supporting further their idea to upkeep SDG#15.

Business Model and SDG#15 Life on Land

In November 2023 members of the family decided to shape their commitment in alignment with international initiatives. After studying the UN SDGs, they revised their approach and rationale on how and what to focus on. They used the IRIS+ tool (https://iris.thegiin.org) as a practical guide to rebuild their business model, indicators, metrics and benchmarks to be able to systematically direct DLO to work towards their goals. Within SDG#15, Table 5.2 shows the management indicators defined for the coming years.

Given the lack of governmental or international support within Honduras, restructuring the business model to manage several SDGs would be supported by internal funding.

Table 5.2. SDG#15 Indicators for DLO.

Target	Impact Category	Impact Theme	Strategic Goal	Key Indicator
15.1 15.2 15.c	Agriculture and biodiversity and ecosystems	Sustainable agriculture and biodiversity & ecosystem conservation	Improving climate resilience through agriculture	Area and percent of land managed using resilient soil health practices
15.4 15.c	Agricultural and biodiversity and ecosystems	Sustainable agriculture and biodiversity & ecosystem conservation	Improving ecosystem health through agriculture	Area of land directly managed by the organisation with an improved biodiversity footprint
15.4 15.5 15.c	Biodiversity and ecosystems	Biodiversity & ecosystem conservation	Improving biodiversity through terrestrial ecosystem protection and restoration	Protected area or restored natural ecosystems Number of species present in the area directly controlled (species richness)
15.9 15.c	Biodiversity and ecosystems	Sustainable agriculture and biodiversity & ecosystem conservation	Improving biodiversity through nature-based solutions and green infrastructure	Area and percent of area directly controlled with improved biodiversity footprint

In 2023, Rebeca participated in representing the company in a Triple Impact Sustainability competition (Social, Economic and Environmental) promoted by the Bank of Central America (BAC), winning first place for their work with impact and the family feel proud because what they are doing in conservation issues has been recognised and rewarded. Recently, in May 2024, an advertisement sponsored by BAC was made where Rebeca shows the impact of the farm.

In 2024, they destined five percent of their budget to work on the triple organizational impact and promote their approach via social media networks and other communication channels.

Reporting and Measurement

As a family in business, members consciously monitor the environmental impact of their projects through defined and strategic activities.

- The farm has been organised and sectioned by crop areas with natural separations such as road, trees and others, thus help to achieve SDG#15.1
- Two large areas of 15 hectares and five hectares have been defined as internal reserves where cultivation is not carried out and the conservation of the environment is maintained. This helps the family business in meeting SDG#15.1, SDG#15.2, SDG#15.4 and SDG#15.5.
- In the crop areas, zero deforestation is respected, which relates to SDG#15.3, and agricultural management practices respect the non-use of agrochemicals, burning, use of herbicides, etc., so that the species of birds, insects and terrestrial animals have a healthy environment and at the same time the agricultural product maintains its healthy and natural conditions. This helps the family business to align itself with SDG#15.1, SDG#15.2, SDG#15.4 and SDG#15.5.

Whilst the crop cultivation and reserve areas have been assigned with specific boundaries DLO is yet to achieve the desired SDG#15 metrics. DLO is committed to formalise the registry of species of birds, terrestrial animals, trees and other fauna in the second half of 2024. This helps the family business to contribute to achieving SDG#15.5 – protect biodiversity and natural habits and SDG#15.9 – integrate ecosystem and biodiversity in government planning.

The family has committed to manage the environmental impact and conservation challenges based on their conviction to steward the resources they have been entrusted with. This commitment, to having a healthy natural environment, impacts on their objective to produce healthy and nutritious products. The Paz family does not, and cannot, see it as two different or separate things. Integrity, as a core value, underpins such commitment, which makes a difference in the way DLO manages their immediate environment to benefit their country and region.

Business and Greater Good

One of the family dreams is to certify their forest as a Natural Reserve Park and establish it as a natural sanctuary in the Lake Yojoa area, aiming to fulfil SDG#15.5 and SDG#15.9. DLO aspires to be known as the business by which others benchmark themselves both in the area and in the country in terms of sustainable agricultural practices with a focus on conservation, giving priority to the flora and fauna. DLO aims to become a centre for visitors to learn about the coexistence between indigenous crops and conservation, therefore helping to meet

SDG#15.c, which aims to 'increase the capacity of lobal communities to purpose sustainable livelihood opportunities' (United Nations, n.d., para.8). In doing so, they aim to educate the consumer that the production and consumption of healthy products goes hand in hand with conservation.

The Paz family want their story to transcend not only in Honduras but worldwide. They have always maintained the concept in the family that DLO is 'A World Class Company' and that they are building the foundation for their family business to meet this goal.

Challenges of Working With SDG#15 Life on Land

The biggest challenge of working on the SDGs and especially SDG#15 is record keeping. SDG#15 requires the scientific and technical contribution of specialists to support them in the identification of the entire environment.

The institutional limitations in Honduras are evident and limiting. There are no governmental or official institutions that can provide guidance on SDGs guidelines. Prior initiatives have failed or are outside of official priority activities. The Paz family have had to look for independent institutions or professionals but due to the high costs associated with such assistance this has been outside of the family businesses financial capacity.

2024 has been set as a starting point due to growth in sales and the opportunity to start exporting. This will generate the possibility of being able to self-finance their SDG objectives. The Paz family will continue investigating other options at a local and international level that can support them on such a journey. 'I am not discouraged, in fact it is another opportunity that will fill us with pride when we start it', says Rebeca Paz, who is deeply in love with the natural environment DLO has established itself in (R. Paz, personal communication, June 1, 2024). As a family, they continue to work in an orderly and schematic manner so as not to lose sight of what environmental responsibility means for generations to come.

'They [birds, squirrels and other fauna] were here before us... and even if they generate some minimal damage to the crop, it is nothing. They continue to deserve respect for their lives' declares Marcio Paz regarding the importance that the family gives to the issue of respect for the ecosystem environment at Finca La Fé (M. Paz, personal communication, June 1, 2024).

What Next for Finca La Fé, Del Lago Orgánico and SDG#15

For DLO, 2024 has been set as the year to capitalise on their exponential sales growth, led by the export of products manufactured in May. The Paz family have prepared to make an investment in processing equipment to meet the demands associated with sales growth and export orders. However, at the farm level, they have decided to no longer expand on cultivation areas and instead preserve the ecosystem that Finca La Fé benefits from. Whilst the current cultivation area can generate only a minimum percentage of raw materials for their final products it can still generate the financial flow that they need to self-finance the implementation of SDGs and especially SDG#15.

The Paz family have reached out to local producers of plantain, cacao, coffee, sweet potato, taro, cassava, etc. who will provide them with the raw materials. DLO will work with them with a focus on the issue of sustainable agricultural practices and to educate them around the conservation of terrestrial life in their farms and future projects. DLO as a family business wish to promote the same principles of zero deforestation, zero agrochemicals, zero burning, zero herbicides and taking care of life that they abide by.

DLO will strongly promote a campaign called 'Preserving the Life of Our Ecosystems.' In doing so they plan for their consumers to become more aware of the importance of producing healthy products, while taking care of life on land, applying ecological principles to take care of the immediate environment. The campaign will be a great challenge but at the same time it is, according to Rebeca Paz, 'a challenge to be transcendental and become agents of change in the country and for new generations. . . .' The Paz family believes they will be able to achieve this as they plan to integrate further their religious faith into DLO operations. Their commercial and conservation approach is based on the Bible, specifically in Proverbs 16:3 (Contemporary English Version) 'Share your plans with the Lord, and you will succeed.'

Family businesses like DLO, showcase that the production of international commodities such as cacao and coffee, can also integrate a strong intergenerational motivation to steward natural resources (Arias & Discua Cruz, 2018; Discua Cruz et al., 2020) and integrate their approach with strong religious convictions shared within and across generations (Discua Cruz & Cavalcanti, 2023). Such an intergenerational approach, where several generations agree on the international initiatives to follow and how best to do it, can support the successful implementation and continuity of the UN SDGs over time.

References

Arias, R. A. C., & Discua Cruz, A. (2018). Rethinking artisan entrepreneurship in a small island: A tale of two chocolatiers in Roatan, Honduras. *International Journal of Entrepreneurial Behavior & Research*, *25*(4), 633–651.

Discua Cruz, A., & Cavalcanti, M. I. (2023). The impact of a Christian perspective on environmental protection and sustainability practices. In A. Singh, M. Vu, & N. Burton (Eds.), *Faith traditions and sustainability: New views and practices for environmental protection* (pp. 39–62). Springer International Publishing.

Discua Cruz, A., Centeno Caffarena, L., & Vega Solano, M. (2020). Being different matters! A closer look into product differentiation in specialty coffee family farms in Central America. *Cross Cultural & Strategic Management*, *27*(2), 165–188.

UNECE. (n.d.). Ecosystem services | UNECE. *UNCE*. https://unece.org/ecosystem-services-0

United Nations. (n.d.). *15: Protect, restore and promote sustainable use of terrestrial ecosystems, sustainably manage forests, combat desertification, and halt and reverse land degradation and halt biodiversity loss*. United Nations: Department of Economic and Social Affairs—Sustainable Development. https://sdgs.un.org/goals/goal15

Chapter 6

Australia: SSS Strawberries – Enhancing Environmental Sustainability

Marina Skinner[a] *and Gina Dang*[b]

[a]Generational Harmony, Australia
[b]SSS Strawberries, Australia

Introduction

Australia is the world's driest inhabited continent on earth. About 20% of Australia is classified as a desert with incredibly high evaporation rates (World Atlas, 2024). There must be an increased focus on efficient irrigation systems, enhanced biodiversity practices, integration of ecosystems and reduction of soil, water and nutrient runoff into local waterways. This means environmental sustainability is a challenge for farmers.

In the heart of Bundaberg, Queensland, SSS Strawberries is a prominent player in the agricultural sector and deeply committed to environmental sustainability. Led by the second generation of the Dang family, SSS Strawberries has flourished into the second largest strawberry growers in Australia. From humble beginnings in Perth with just five acres, they have sown the seeds of success, cultivating over 300 acres and more than four million strawberry plants, becoming a cornerstone of the region's employment with over 350 dedicated staff during peak seasons.

Products and Services Offered by the Family Business

SSS Strawberries supplies fresh strawberries predominantly for Woolworths and Aldi supermarkets and sells direct to the public from the farm. They also produce and export frozen and freeze-dried strawberries to Vietnam, South Korea and the United States (US) marketed through Gina's Table, a member of the SSS Strawberries Group. They are also exploring new markets in Japan, Taiwan, the European Union (EU) and the United Kingdom (UK). Table 6.1 identifies the products and other activities performed by the SSS Strawberries Group.

Attaining the 2030 Sustainable Development Goal of Life on Land, 67–81
doi:10.1108/978-1-83608-212-520241006

Table 6.1. Products and Services Provided by SSS Strawberries.

Products	Other Activities
Fresh strawberries	Retail – Strawberry store (on-site)
Freeze dried fruit snacks	Farm tours
Happles™ apple dusted fruit	
Merries™ berries	Pick your own strawberries
Frozen fruits	Manufacturing
Freeze dried fruit powders	Accommodation
Freeze dried fruit crumbles	Property development

SSS Strawberries is an innovator in value-adding through the adoption of freeze-drying technology to recycle damaged or excess fruit into a brand-new packaged retail product Happles™, Merries™ and frozen marketed as Gina's Table. There are also significant environmental benefits through the reduction of waste which align with their sustainability vision.

> It's heart-breaking to watch fruit that we have grown get rejected and destroyed. We wanted to find a way to ensure that the fruit, that can't be sold due to strict criteria, has a second-life. The level of innovation now available in freeze-dried technology has allowed us to take the next steps in value adding to tonnes of strawberries that may have ended up rejected and destroyed in the past due to market conditions. (Dang, 2023, as cited in Haupt, 2023, para. 3-4)

Freeze drying is the process where frozen raw materials are placed in a refrigerated vacuum, and ice crystals in the product are sublimated into water vapour, while the cell structure of the original product remains. SSS Strawberries ensured that the technology delivered on its sustainability goals and the supplier, Gesellschaft für Entstaubungs-Anlagen mbH (GEA), also aligned and upheld the same values as SSS Strawberries. The GEA freeze-drying machine (Fig. 6.1), sourced from Denmark, is located inside a 4,000 m² purpose-built facility at SSS Strawberries. It can process more than 2,000 tonnes of fruit.

SSS Strawberries invested in the factory to help end food waste and push forward into its next phase of development. The new freeze-drying technology also allows for a variety of production applications such as frozen fruit, powders, crumbles and healthy snacks on-the-go.

> It also helps growers like ourselves to create new and interesting product lines for both the Australian market and our export markets. Freeze dried fruits retain their nutritional value, shape integrity, are lightweight, have a long shelf life, are genetically modified organism (GMO) free and all natural, and most importantly, it not only keeps but intensifies the flavour. (Dang, 2023, as cited in Haupt, 2023, para.7)

Fig. 6.1.   The GEA Freeze-Drying Machine Allows for a Variety of Production Applications. *Source:* SSS Strawberries (2024).

Bundaberg Mayor Jack Dempsey says

> The global food supply stemming from the Bundaberg Region's 'food bowl' perfectly combines its natural competitive advantage with state-of-the-art food processing. (Dempsey, 2023, as cited in Haupt, 2023, para.9)

SSS Strawberries also expanded its product line, opening The Strawberry Shop in May 2023 and secured the intellectual property across 29 countries of Happles™ and Gina's Table™, an additive-free Australian-made freeze-dried snack, available nationwide. With the opening of a new 210-acre farm, the business' growth is intertwined with its community's well-being and prosperity.

Vision, Mission, Values and Philosophy

SSS Strawberries envisions a world where

- every meal is a celebration of sustainability,
- every farmer stands tall and
- every plate tells a story of hope and success.

This dream took root and is nurtured by the Dang family's unwavering commitment to family, excellence and people-first values. These values are the foundation of SSS Strawberries' success and underpins its business culture. Their guiding principle centres around prioritising family and this approach, instilled in them from an early age, influences all their actions. By sharing core values and pursuing a shared objective, they successfully manage the demands of both family and business. Additionally, perseverance is a fundamental value within their family (Hartman, 2024).

> As a family, we also support each other no matter what. Our mum told us that no matter the situation, we must stick together as she taught us '*One chopstick can easily break, but a bunch is much harder to break*'. (Dang, 2024, as cited in Hartman, 2024, para.45)

This guiding philosophy has fostered a robust family unit and management team within SSS Strawberries, all aligned in pursuit of a shared objective. Such cohesion is uniquely achievable in a family business, providing a substantial competitive edge. To deliver on its dream, SSS Strawberries' mission as primary producers and food manufacturers is to promote healthy and sustainable food.

Background to the Family and the Business

Led by the second generation of the Dang family – Victor, Thanh, Toan, Lily, Gina, Cindy, Trinity and Rena – SSS Strawberries has flourished (see Fig. 6.2). The 'SSS' in SSS Strawberries stands for 'Seven Successful Siblings', as all seven siblings hold key leadership roles in the business and sit on the Board. Gem Nguyen, their mother, is the influential engine behind the operation, holding an advisory role.

Fig. 6.2.   Dang Family Source: SSS Strawberries. *Source:* Gina Dang.

The Dang family has an incredible drive and work ethic which underpins the business' growth and resilience. Their parents had a natural talent for entrepreneurship, based on their ability to withstand even the toughest challenges, and they've passed this onto their children. The family story is one of inspiration and determination to create a better life for the entire Dang family, after experiencing the aftermath of the Vietnam War, as the Historical Timeline illustrates (see Fig. 6.3).

The Dang family, originally from Vietnam, endured numerous hardships including failed escape attempts by their father resulting in imprisonment, punishment and torture. Their mother successfully negotiated his release and the family, including 6 children under 10, fled Vietnam. They endured a tough journey by boat to Indonesia during which food and water was stolen by other ships. Whilst at the refugee camp, refugee applications were initially rejected. To survive, they ran several businesses as builders, farmers, bakers, and wine makers and established the first Asian supermarket in their region in Indonesia, with ingenuity and limited resources.

Eventually, they were sponsored by an Australian family, the Franklins, and successfully resettled in Perth in 1994. After the family made it to Australia, despite language barriers and financial struggles, they worked as pickers and packers on strawberry farms. In 2000, the parents leased five acres of land from a friend and began their own strawberry farm which would eventually become SSS Strawberries. They began selling seconds-quality strawberries to Asian grocers and fruit and vegetable shops. This was their first business in Australia, and all the children were actively involved in it – sitting on the floor cutting strawberries and putting them in takeaway containers to be delivered to stores.

Although the first few seasons were not profitable, due to poor quality and low market prices, they built a relationship with an exporter in their third year and leased another 10 acres of land to serve the export market. The business turned a profit in the fourth season, when the children began to help with bookkeeping and money management, by paying down their debt and diverting funds to the export market. Two years later, the entire family and business moved to Bundaberg, Queensland, where they purchased 82 acres of farmland. Due to the timing of the Queensland strawberry season, the Dang family discovered they could earn four times as much per punnet.

The first year in Queensland was very challenging as they had invested everything into the new farm and the crops failed. They were $2.1 million in debt with no income and were unable to employ staff. The entire family worked from sunrise to sunset. As each year passed, things slowly began to improve. They refined processes, grew the team and became profitable. By 2019, they were able to purchase a second farm and doubled the size of the business. SSS Strawberries now achieves $20+ million in revenue per year.

The family's determination to provide for themselves and create a friendly working environment for others was a key factor in its success. Unlike the rest of the industry, SSS Strawberries has a reputation for treating workers like family and providing fair work conditions.

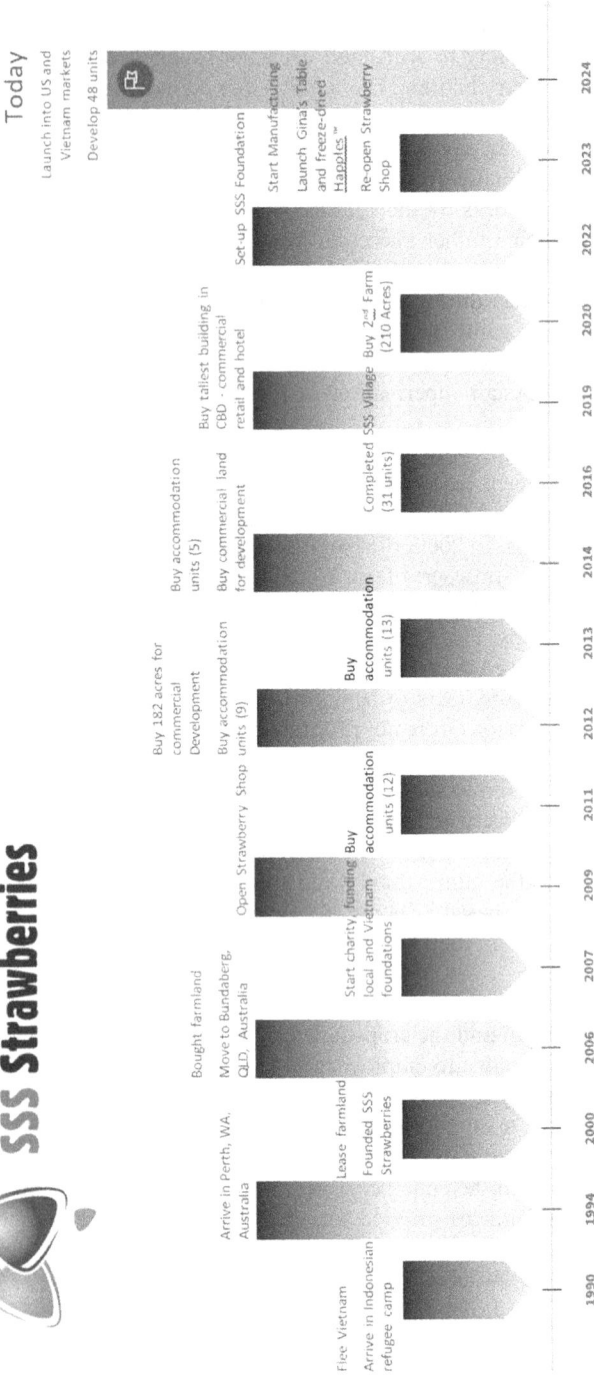

Fig. 6.3.   Historical Timeline. *Source:* Authors own.

Had the business not been a family business, we most likely would have failed. Our family has seen the business through the darkest times and we siblings have worked in the business since we were children, sometimes from sunrise to sunset and often performing extremely physically demanding work. It's difficult to replicate that unrelenting drive and focus in a business that isn't a family business. (G. Dang, personal communication, August 7, 2022)

The Dang family has an unrivalled drive, entrepreneurial spirit and persistence borne from intense struggles. The founders had to start over again and again. Their story is a testament to the family's resilience, innovation and persistence. With the help of their seven children, they built SSS Strawberries from the ground up.

Meet the SSS Strawberry Family

First Generation
    Tan Dang – Retired and
    Gem Nguyen – Oversees the farm

Second Generation
    Victor Dang – Chief Executive Officer (CEO),
    Toan Nguyen – Group Chief Financial Officer (CFO),
    Gina Dang – General Manager/CEO and Founder of Gina's Table,
    Thanh Dang – Chief Marketing Officer (CMO),
    Lily Dang – Retail Manager,
    Trinity Dang – Internal and Global Relationship Manager,
    Cindy Dang – Property Manager and
    Rena Dang – Human Resources (HR) Manager.

Each of the siblings has sought tertiary qualifications. As the business grew, they became more strategic and identified gaps in knowledge and expertise required to add value to the growth of the business. They all demonstrate a strong background and experience in their respective disciplines adding to the leadership team's diverse expertise and business acumen.

SDG#15: Life on Land and SSS Strawberries

SSS Strawberries' practices align with its vision and strategy, delivering on several targets of the Sustainable Development Goal 15 (SDG#15), 'Life on Land,' particularly focusing on sustainable land management, combating desertification, protecting biodiversity and integrating ecosystem and biodiversity values into planning and development processes. This case elaborates on how SSS Strawberries contributes to the following SDG#15 targets: 15.1, 15.3, 15.5, 15.6, 15.8, 15.9 and 15.a.

SDG#15.3: End Desertification and Restore Degraded Land

SSS Strawberries has adopted a multi-faceted approach to combat desertification and restore degraded land, which includes sustainable farming practices and advanced irrigation techniques. It is committed to sustainable land use that contributes to a land degradation-neutral world, ensuring the strawberry fields remain productive and resilient.

Sustainable Farming Practices

One of the cornerstone practices at SSS Strawberries is maintaining soil health through organic farming methods. Mulches and cover crops are used to protect the soil, enhance its fertility and prevent erosion, which is aligned with SDG#15.3. During the processing of Happles™, all the biproducts such as apple cores, strawberry leaves and tops are converted into compost for farm use. These practices are crucial in areas susceptible to desertification, as they help maintain the soil structure and moisture levels necessary for sustainable agriculture. By employing crop rotation and reduced tillage methods, SSS Strawberries minimises soil disturbance, which helps to preserve soil integrity and reduce erosion. These techniques also enhance soil biodiversity and resilience, making the land more resistant to the impacts of climate change and extreme weather events.

Advanced Irrigation Techniques

Water management is another critical aspect of SSS Strawberries' strategy to combat desertification. Water tanks have been installed, and the land surrounding the factory has been landscaped to allow wastewater to be used for watering the grass and trees. SSS Strawberries strive to ensure the conservation, restoration and sustainable use of terrestrial and inland freshwater ecosystems, aligned with SDG#15.1, recognising obligations to safeguard these vital ecosystems. Drip irrigation systems deliver water directly to the plant roots, thereby reducing wastage and ensuring efficient water use. This method is particularly effective in sustainable water management where scarcity is a significant concern. Additionally, SSS Strawberries employs soil moisture sensors to monitor and precisely manage irrigation needs. This technology optimises water use, prevents over-irrigation and avoids soil salinisation which can degrade land and make it unsuitable for agriculture.

SDG#15.5: Protect Biodiversity and Natural Habitats

SSS Strawberries' commitment to biodiversity conservation is evident in its farming practices and community engagement initiatives. With a focus on creating and maintaining healthy ecosystems that support a wider farming region, these strawberry fields and surrounding shelterbelts (Sustainable Farms, 2024) play a crucial role in protecting crops. They also serve as natural corridors and habitats for various wildlife.

Farming practices are employed to promote healthy and natural pesticide methods and fertilisers that are not harmful to wildlife and do not degrade habitats. These practices help to preserve the area's natural biodiversity and protect wildlife habitats.

Integrated Pest Management (IPM) is a core component of SSS Strawberries' strategy used to maintain soil and plant health. IPM involves monitoring pest populations and using targeted biological controls, such as beneficial insects, to manage pests naturally. This approach reduces the need for chemical interventions and helps maintain a balanced ecosystem on the farm.

SDG#15.6: Promote Access to Genetic Resources and Fair Sharing of Benefits

SSS Strawberries invests in research and development and partners with agricultural research institutions to develop new farming methods and create new crop varieties that are resilient to pests, diseases and climate change. By participating in such initiatives, SSS Strawberries contributes to the global effort to ensure that genetic resources are used sustainably and equitably. It also supports local farmers to enhance agricultural productivity and sustainability. Every strawberry season, it reserves and delegates an area of the farm to trial and test new varieties. It shares these research findings with local farmers and the industry to improve overall crop yields.

SDG#15.8: Prevent Invasive Alien Species on Land and in Water Ecosystems

Biosecurity Measures

SSS Strawberries has established strict biosecurity protocols to prevent the introduction of invasive species. These protocols include regular monitoring of plant health, stringent sanitation measures and the use of certified disease-free planting materials. By maintaining a controlled farming environment, it reduces the risk of introducing non-native species that could disrupt local ecosystems.

Use of Native Plants and Natural Pest Control

As previously mentioned in SDG#15.5, natural pest control methods are a key part of SSS Strawberries' strategy. By using beneficial insects and other biological controls where possible, they manage pest populations without resorting to chemical pesticides that can harm non-target species and disrupt the delicate balance of the ecosystem. Its dedication ensures the health of the strawberry farms and surrounding areas.

Collaboration with Industries and Associations

As noted in SDG#15.6, SSS Strawberries' collaborations with industry and associations involve research and development, sharing knowledge and resources. By working together with other stakeholders, SSS Strawberries helps to protect local ecosystems, maintain biodiversity and implement effective strategies to manage water use, pests and diseases.

SDG#15.9: Integrate Ecosystem and Biodiversity in Governmental Planning

SSS Strawberries actively engages with local governments and associations to promote policies and practices that support ecosystem and biodiversity conservation. Integrating ecosystem and biodiversity values into national and local planning processes is essential for sustainable development.

Advocacy for Sustainable Policies

SSS Strawberries advocates for policies that support sustainable agriculture. It actively participates in regional planning processes and provides input on policy development, ensuring that environmental factors are considered in decision-making. It strives to create a supportive framework for sustainable development.

SDG#15.a: Increase Financial Resources to Conserve and Sustainably Use Ecosystems

Mobilising financial resources to conserve and sustainably use ecosystems is crucial to achieve SDG#15.a. SSS Strawberries has made significant investments in technologies and practices that promote sustainable ecosystem management. To assist the achievement of SDG#15.a, SSS Strawberries has invested in state-of-the-art technologies that enhance the sustainability of its operations. For example, the freeze-drying and freezing facilities enables the processing of surplus unmarketable produce to reduce food waste. By minimising waste, these technologies contribute to the sustainable use of local agricultural resources and reduce the environmental impact of its operations and those of other farmers. As a family member says, 'this isn't just a business endeavour; it's a step towards a more sustainable future for our region and beyond' (SSS Strawberries, 2024, para. 6).

Business Model and SDG#15 and Other Sustainable Development Goals

SSS Strawberries is constantly evolving to capitalise on opportunity and minimise risk by proactively seeking out methods to create value for the business and stakeholders, whilst enhancing its environmental sustainability. Farming is a high-risk sector with several factors influencing profitability that are out of the business' control. Bad weather is a constant concern as it can mean the difference between a successful and failed crop. The COVID-19 pandemic created new risks including a lack of demand due to lockdowns and a shortage of pickers and packers available to harvest crops. The biggest risk faced in farming is the inability to set the market price. Recognising these risks, the business sets strategy with a long-term view, pivoting when required and continually monitoring, measuring and reviewing. For example, the whole business moved from Perth to Bundaberg in search of greater opportunities.

SSS Strawberries have diversified into real estate and launched a factory for high-tech freeze-dried food processing, aligning with SDG#9: Industry, Innovation and Infrastructure, as a value-add to the sustainability processes already employed with SDG#15 targets. The factory enables it to transform fresh second-grade produce into crunchy freeze-dried snacks and a strawberry powder for natural flavouring and colouring. Aligning with SDG#12: Responsible Consumption and Production, any strawberries that are under/over size or damaged (out-of-specification) are transformed into a new product to supply the market year-round. This reduces waste by about 300 tonnes/year, reducing the burden on landfill and saving the business approximately $600,000 in wasted labour and disposal costs with the added potential to earn $300,000 in revenue.

The Bundaberg region produces almost one billion dollars in fruit, vegetables and nuts each year. SSS Strawberries partners with other local growers to freeze-dry their produce, thereby enhancing SDG#17: Partnerships for the Goals. This contributes significantly to the business' success and provides flow-on benefits for the agricultural sector and related industries. The upcycling opportunities of its freeze-drying facility brings a greater benefit to the region. On top of supporting other farmers upcycling their unmarketable fruits and vegetables, SSS Strawberries is helping the region to reduce thousands of tons of out-of-specification products annually, thereby reducing losses and bringing profits to farmers.

> We have engaged in several strategic collaborations to enhance the sustainability and reach of our freeze-drying initiative. One notable partnership is with a large apple grower in Victoria, also raspberry and blueberry farmers in our local region which led to the development of the innovative Happles™ product range. This venture showcases our commitment to collaborative product innovation. (Dang, 2024, as cited in Hartman, 2024, para. 33)

Through the adoption of freeze-drying techniques, SSS Strawberries is maximising food use and supporting SDG# 2: Zero Hunger. It means fresh fruits are freeze-dried at their seasonal best, are healthy and nutritious, lightweight and can easily be exported. Unlike transporting fresh fruits that require refrigeration, freeze-dried fruits can be stored at ambient room temperatures and weigh less which helps to reduce energy and fuel consumption from refrigeration storage and transportation. Lower 'food miles' further reduce their carbon footprint. SSS Strawberries' ability to process its and other local producers' food waste onsite lessens or eliminates the distance involved if the food were sent to landfill. This spurred the creation of the Gina's Table brand, which isn't just about avoiding waste, it's about embracing a circular economy that benefits everyone – from local farmers to global consumers.

Contributions to achieving SDG#8: Decent work and Economic Growth and SDG#11: Sustainable Cities and Communities are demonstrated with SSS Strawberries' unique contribution to community when they developed a purpose-built SSS Village for its workers. The 30-unit purpose-built village, which houses 240 residents at a low-cost, has helped to prevent any worker shortages, even throughout COVID-19. The goal was to provide a home away from home, improving employee satisfaction and increasing productivity rates. Up to 50 new jobs were created by providing safe, sustainable housing and working conditions. SSS Strawberries bolsters economic growth and offers fair work. As a family business, SSS Strawberries prioritises the health, well-being and happiness of all employees by treating them like part of their family. It employs a diverse and transient workforce, including many international fruit pickers and are sensitive to their specific needs.

> We celebrate and accept different cultures, recognizing the unique contributions each individual brings to our team. As Vietnamese immigrants ourselves, we celebrate our cultural milestones and ensure everyone in the organisation has the opportunity to celebrate their own cultural events. This inclusive approach fosters a supportive and welcoming environment for all employees. We strive to create a workplace culture that embraces diversity in all its forms, ensuring that every individual feels like a valued member of our family. By promoting openness and understanding, we ensure that all employees feel a sense of belonging and support. (G. Dang, personal communication, May 16, 2024)

SSS Strawberries holds regular training and communication with its employees and addresses any unconscious biases, fostering an equitable workplace where decisions are made based on merit and inclusivity. This initiative is crucial in maintaining its family-first ethos. SSS Strawberries is committed to creating a workplace where diversity is celebrated, and everyone can thrive. Its strategy is not just about policies but also about nurturing a supportive and empowering family atmosphere for all and for the business to operate with a circular economy intent. SSS Strawberries recognises integrating SDG's into their business strategies can significantly enhance their return on investment (ROI) by managing risks, reducing costs, fostering innovation, improving employee engagement and building customer loyalty. These benefits are measurable and contribute to sustainable growth and long-term profitability.

Challenges of Working With SDG#15 and SSS Strawberries

Food sustainability presents a pressing global challenge. Approximately, one-third of all food produced worldwide is lost or wasted, while over three billion people struggle to afford healthy diets. This issue becomes even more critical as the global population continues to rise. By 2050, an estimated 2 billion more people will inhabit the planet, necessitating sustainable solutions to meet their food needs without compromising valuable forests (IMPAAKT, 2024).

Reducing food wastage by SSS Strawberries has been achieved through the 2023 launch of the largest commercial high-tech freeze-drying factory in Australia. Together with Happles™ and Merries™, it has secured exports. SSS Strawberries has also continued to build its global business network with a partly government funded research trip to the EU, informing its plans to export food products into the European market. Research and development into global expansion to export fresh strawberries into the EU market during Australia's peak production months has been a success and further international markets are now being explored.

The social impact of SSS Strawberries' work tackles the challenge of excessive food waste due to supermarket standards demanding cosmetically perfect produce. This results in vast quantities of edible food being discarded, costing farmers money and impacting the environment significantly as edible produce is sent to landfill, creating methane. As food prices soar amidst a cost-of-living crisis, SSS Strawberries food waste reduction initiative seeks to help themselves and other primary producers in repurposing rejected produce into high-quality, profitable goods while aligning with the National Food Waste Strategy to halve Australia's food waste by 2030 and mitigate unnecessary economic losses and land usage.

Awards

SSS Strawberries has been recognised with numerous awards for its exceptional achievements and contributions in Australia and internationally.

2022 Gold Asia Pacific Stevie Award – Excellence in Innovation
2022 International Business Award – Company of the Year (Consumer Products)
2022 Family Business Excellence Award – Medium Business (Family Business Association: State and National levels, Australia and New Zealand)
2022 Finalist Ethnic Business Award (Medium to Large Business)
2022 Silver AusMumpreneur Award (Queensland/Northern Territory, Australia)
2023 Distinguished Family Business of the Year Awards – Family Business Association (Australia and New Zealand)
2024 Finalist Banksia Sustainability Award
2024 Shortlisted World Food Innovation Award
2024 Gold Clean + Conscious Award for snacks & Best Low Waste Food Product category
2024 ABA100 Winner for Eco Innovation in The Australian Brand Awards
2025 Silver International Business Awards in Sustainability Leadership Award.

Business and Greater Good

SSS Strawberries also values the importance of giving back. It is dedicated to improving the community, which is why the SSS Foundation was established. Its generosity extends beyond the local community and back to the family's homeland and those less fortunate. The Dang family believes its success is intertwined with the community's well-being and prosperity.

> We build homes, bridges, water wells and provide financial support to orphanages in Vietnam and the Philippines and funded cataract surgeries for those less fortunate in Vietnam. This is in addition to assisting local charities, hospitals, schools, and clubs. In total we have contributed around $100,000 towards these causes. Our parents have always valued giving back to the community, volunteering at Caodaist temples and with farmers before they got their start. (G. Dang, personal communication, May 16, 2024)

What Next for SSS Strawberries and SDG#15

The SSS Strawberries' journey continues with exciting developments and in line with its strategy for sustainability, SSS Strawberries is always looking ahead. It is

- … in the process of installing solar panels to offset a substantial portion of the energy needs of their facility,
- … considering the possibility of energy storage solutions, such as batteries, to capture excess solar energy generated
- … working towards finding a packaging solution that is recycled and low waste (Currently, it uses aluminium packaging due to the high moisture barrier that freeze-dried fruit requires to maintain its quality, integrity and shelf life)
- … addressing Australia's housing crisis with the largest unit development in the Wide Bay region in Queensland, Australia.

Synonymous with global population growth is a need for more environmentally sustainable housing and high-density developments that reduce land use. The business already has a purpose-built 'SSS Village', which not only provides high-density affordable housing but also resolved the issue of previous worker shortages during peak strawberry seasons. SSS Strawberries has added 17 commercial and residential properties to its 60-strong real estate portfolio, with another 48 units built in March 2023.

SSS Strawberries owns the tallest commercial building in the city of Bundaberg, SSS Tower, and is collaborating with Local Government to address accommodation shortages. Discussions include rezoning the area to supply 450 high-density housing lots, a seven-storey airport apartment hotel and a seven-storey student accommodation block with commercial facilities, the most significant development in the Bundaberg CBD in 30 years.

As SSS Strawberries grows, the business remains dedicated to its values, family and the Bundaberg community. Its story is not just about surviving challenges – it's about thriving and enhancing environmental sustainability to make a lasting global impact.

References

Hartman, J. (2024, February 29). Gina Dang on 5 things you need to run a highly successful family business. *Authority Magazine*. https://medium.com/authority-magazine/gina-dang-on-5-things-you-need-to-run-a-highly-successful-family-business-c100df671425

Haupt, P. (2023). Freeze drying factory opens in Bundaberg. *Food & Drink Business*. https://www.foodanddrinkbusiness.com.au/news/freeze-drying-factory-opens-in-bundaberg

IMPAAKT. (2024). SSS strawberries: IMPAAKT's most iconic food sustainability company of 2024. *IMPAAKT*. https://impaakt.co/sss-strawberries-impaakts-most-iconic-food-sustainability-company-of-2024/

SSS Strawberries. (2024). The SSS strawberry story. *SSS Strawberries*. https://sss-strawberries.com.au/about-us/

Sustainable Farms. (2024). Managing natural assets on farms: Shelterbelts. *Sustainable Farms*. https://www.sustainablefarms.org.au/wp-content/uploads/2022/09/Shelterbelts-Brochure-FINAL_Feb-2023_online.pdf

World Atlas. (2024). The World's Driest Continent. *World Facts*. https://www.worldatlas.com/articles/which-is-the-world-s-driest-continent.html

Chapter 7

Australia: Family Business and Life on Land – The Case of SOILCO

Mary Barrett

University of Wollongong, Australia

Introduction

SOILCO designs, builds and operates organics recycling facilities. Using proven technologies, the company transforms organic resources into quality-assured compost and mulch products that regenerate and give life to soil. SOILCO prides itself on enabling the circular economy by harnessing the power of people and technology. The company's activities – aided by its family business ethos – precisely evoke SDG#15: the company improves life *on* the land – in fact it improves the life *of* the land – by returning to the soil nutrients that are made available in the form of waste collected by individuals, businesses and city councils. SOILCO operates in five locations in two Australian states: New South Wales and Australian Capital Territory. In New South Wales, the locations are Nowra, Kembla Grange and Tweed Heads. SOILCO is developing greenfield sites in New South Wales and Queensland, including projects in Sydney and Brisbane.

The Wogamia composting facility, located in West Nowra, NSW, was the first SOILCO site to recycle organics. SOILCO has been processing garden and timber waste there since 2001 and further infrastructure improvements were completed in 2018. The Kembla Grange compost manufacturing facility located in Wollongong NSW processes food, garden and timber waste. Along with sorting, shredding and screening, SOILCO uses in-vessel composting (IVC) technology which maximises processing capacity, increasing final output with minimal footprint requirements. Badgerys Creek (Western Sydney) is one of three greenfield sites SOILCO secured in 2022 and 2023 for development into large-scale organics recovery facilities. In 2024, the combined capacity of the greenfield projects was predicted to exceed 500,000 tonnes per annum. SOILCO's Tweed Heads Organics Processing Facility is located at Stotts Creek Resource Recovery Centre in the Northern Rivers area of NSW. It can process 25,000 tonnes per annum of food and garden waste into

Attaining the 2030 Sustainable Development Goal of Life on Land, 83–96
Copyright © 2025 Mary Barrett
Published under exclusive licence by Emerald Publishing Limited
doi:10.1108/978-1-83608-212-520241007

quality assured compost for re-use. The Tweed Heads facility uses IVC technology (see below for a brief explanation).[1]

Each site has been strategically located to meet the infrastructure needs of the surrounding region as councils and businesses increasingly move to separate their organic sources for recycling. The technologies for each location are site-specific to meet the planning and operational requirements of the area. Fig. 7.1 summarises the SOILCO business.

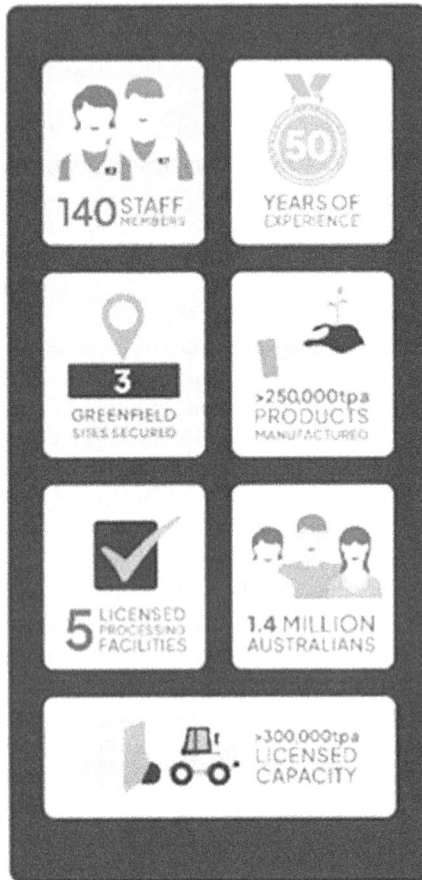

Fig. 7.1.   SOILCO at a Glance. *Source:* SOILCO (2024a).

---

[1]See SOILCO's video about IVC at https://soilco.com.au/services/recycling/tweed-heads/.

SOILCO's Products and Services

Products

SOILCO manufactures a range of general purpose and specific growing soil mixes that meet Australian quality standards for general purpose soils, topdressing, topsoils and landscaping mixes. Adhering to a quality standard assures customers that the company's soils can grow and maintain plants. The ingredients of SOILCO soil blends include natural soil and certified composts. The natural soil is certified as Virgin Extracted Natural Material (VENM), which means it is free from contaminants generated by industrial, commercial, mining or agricultural activities.

Compost products are also available. Compost enhances overall soil health and improve its resilience to drought. It also increases water absorption, improves drainage and provides slow release of essential nutrients. Compost feeds the soil's micro-organisms and its macro-fauna such as earthworms which process soil, aerating it and creating pathways for water and nutrients. Soil which is well populated with earthworms reduces dependence on inorganic fertilisers and supplemental water and pesticides. In this way, SOILCO's activities support SDG#15's overall goal of halting biodiversity loss.

Mulches derived from timber (woodchips, offcuts, wood shavings and pallets) and composted garden organics free from weed seeds, pests and diseases are another valuable product. Mulches protect the soil surface, beautify the garden and highlight plants. Mulching reduces evaporation from soil, suppresses weeds, protects seedlings from winds, extreme temperatures and raindrop impact, all of which strengthens plant seedlings and increases their survival rates. As mulch breaks down it provides carbon, which builds soil health and supplies food to microbes.

Services

SOILCO also offers waste collection and recycling services for garden, timber and food waste using facilities licenced by the Environmental Protection Authority (EPA). SOILCO accepts organic waste, drilling mud and VENM soil from authorised commercial customers, enabling clients to reduce their waste disposal fees and effectively 'close the loop', that is, return to the soil the materials originally taken from it and so reducing the amount of material going to landfill. This is the circular economy in its most fundamental form.

Businesses also appreciate the benefits to their public image that come from recycling, reducing their carbon footprint and diverting organic waste away from the general waste stream. Food waste recycling, as enabled by the Food Organics and Garden Organics (FOGO) scheme in Wollongong, NSW, is proving popular in some Australian cities where people are increasingly enthusiastic about reducing their waste. People's attitudes make a difference to how successfully household waste recycling works. As Charlie Emery, the Managing Director of SOILCO, puts it:

In parts of the country where people have actually lobbied their local council to introduce food waste reduction methods like FOGO, you find people are better at reducing food waste and sorting rubbish into the correct bins. This means we (SOILCO) can produce a superior product. (C. Emery, personal communication, June 14, 2024)

Clients such as local councils who want to convert a site into, say, a playground can have SOILCO arrange for and coordinate all phases of soil regeneration. This and all SOILCO's operations directly align with SDG#15's goals to:

[...] protect, restore and promote sustainable use of terrestrial ecosystems, sustainably manage forests, combat desertification, and halt and reverse land degradation and halt biodiversity loss. (United Nations, n.d., para.1)

Composting promotes the sustainability of ecosystems by returning resources to the soil. This in turn reverses land degradation and biodiversity loss – microbes and other organisms such as earthworms are, after all, the micro- and macro-fauna of soil. These hidden life forms need to be preserved as much as the endangered species that we are more familiar with because they live on top of the soil.

Technology

SOILCO's technologies are deliberately diverse and fit-for-purpose. The business uses networks which make it possible to manage seasonality without compromising product quality or range. Rather than developing its own intellectual property, SOILCO uses proven techniques from overseas and adapts them to the individual requirements of its sites in Australia. Accordingly, SOILCO uses different composting techniques across a range of Australian sites which vary greatly in their climactic conditions and soil characteristics.

Composting techniques can be clustered into two main groups: aerobic and anaerobic. Aerobic composting refers to composting in the presence of oxygen. It can be done in a variety of ways. IVC, for example, confines the composting materials (waste with vegetable origins) within a building, container or vessel. SOILCO's in-vessel tunnels are individually controlled and use forced aeration and mechanical turning techniques to accelerate composting. The fully automated process allows the operator to set parameters for different waste streams and seasonal fluctuations. Modular construction and versatile control software allow optimal composting conditions.

Anaerobic digestion technology, by contrast, processes organic waste in the absence of oxygen. Waste materials may include food, even bones. As micro-organisms break down the waste, they generate a biogas that can be used as a renewable energy source. The remaining material (digestate) can be composted and used as a fertiliser. SOILCO is currently seeking approval for dry anaerobic digestion technology at some of its greenfield sites, including its proposed Badgerys Creek Clean Energy Compost Manufacturing Facility (CECMF). The CECMF's anaerobic digesters will be able to accept up to 40,000 tonnes per annum of organic waste to produce renewable biogas. This biogas will then be used to produce most of the energy required to run the facility. Again, the circular economy is in evidence.

As noted earlier, SOILCO's processes at its various sites vary greatly. This means that while SOILCO might appear to be technically a simple business in fact the opposite is true. Products and processes carried out at each site differ according to the existing topography and soil type, climactic conditions, the proximity of the SOILCO operation to residences, contractual matters, council requirements and so on. As Charlie Emery put it:

> It would be simple if SOILCO's composting was like Visy making boxes. You could have the same process and make the same thing everywhere. But that's not how composting works. (C. Emery, personal communication, 14 June, 2024)

Managing operations on such different sites and with such different techniques requires precise monitoring and control. Charlie Emery describes SOILCO as 'a highly data-driven organization.' It relies on an integrated and automated Supervisory Control and Data Acquisition (SCADA) system which provides real-time data for all its composting operations.

Vision and Mission

SOILCO's vision is to manage state of the art organics recycling facilities that produce innovative and world's best products and services that meet the soil improvement needs of Eastern Australian communities (SOILCO, 2024b). The company's mission is to transform organic resources into the world's best products to regenerate and enhance the health and productivity of soil and to maximise [its] contribution to clean energy and sustainable communities (SOILCO, 2024b). More poetically and passionately, the SOILCO Manifesto sets out the business's reason for being:

The SOILCO Manifesto

Soil is life giving.

It puts food on our plates.

It purifies our water.

It protects us against flooding and combats drought.

It captures and stores vast amounts of carbon.

Soil is used to make lots of things, from ceramics to skincare, paper to bricks.

It is alive, teeming with microbes that are used in almost all of the antibiotics we take to help fight infection.

It is the foundation of our buildings, roads, houses, and schools.

Soil, like oil and gas, is a finite resource.

It can take up to 400 years for nature to form just one centimetre.

But in just 60 years, the UN predicts a catastrophic loss of fertile land.

Set against a burgeoning population, the threat to our way of life is very real.

At SOILCO, we give life to soil.

Our advanced technologies transform organics into high-quality, enriched soil.

So next time you throw your organic waste into the green bin, think about what it could actually be turned into...

Your apple core could be the solution to fight the next pandemic

Your coffee grinds could be the pages of your child's favourite bedtime book

Your eggshells could be the way to combat carbon emissions

Your chicken bones could be turned into green energy

Your lawn clippings could become the grass pitch upon which your child scores their first goal

And the leftovers from your last meal?

They could grow Australia's finest produce to inspire our next Michelin Star chef.

At SOILCO, we see the life-giving potential that soil holds.

Join us in helping others see its potential too. (SOILCO, 2024c)

All three statements attest to SOILCO's investment in the goals of renewability and sustainability set out in SDG#15. But in its very early days, SOILCO did not look like a business that would be immediately recognisable as 'the life-giving soil company', its current brand. Understanding the background to the family and the business makes it clear how this commitment developed.

Background to the Family and the Business

SOILCO began on the dairy farm operated by Charlie Emery's grandfather. As well as supplying milk, Charlie's grandfather carried out some soil extraction operations in the 1970s more or less as a hobby. Following deregulation of the dairy industry, Charlie's father, Tony Emery, and Tony's brother realized that the dairy farm could not provide both their families with a living. Accordingly, in the 1980s Tony and his wife Maria Emery decided to focus on the soil extraction business. Tony found a water source which was – and still is – used for irrigation on the farm and created a large quarry void. He also found a good seam of sand which he began extracting and selling to a local contractor. Tony also had a couple of trucks. According to Charlie, Tony was always an enthusiastic 'revhead' and had always enjoyed trucks over cattle. Tony had used the trucks to extend the business to include some haulage and other trucking activities. He also used them to shift soil to customers.

Embarrassingly, the sand seam ran out during a major project for a client, and Tony realized that there was in fact more soil than sand. While the soil was reasonably good, it needed enrichment, namely compost, to be suitable for multiple purposes. Tony obtained sludge from a local paper mill and used that to make compost. Shortly afterwards, the Wollongong City Council banned green waste from its waste disposal sites, and this became another source of material for composting. In the late 1990s and early 2000s kerbside recycling was introduced in the Wollongong area and Tony also tapped into this source for compostable material. These two moves typify SOILCO's strategic approach: the business has always closely watched developments in government policy around waste management and been nimble enough to develop opportunities from them.

The following timeline summarises SOILCO's development since it was founded.

Year	Event
1974	The Emery family begin selling soil from a dairy property and buy a truck for deliveries in the Illawarra Shoalhaven region.
1980	The Wogamia Sand Quarry is developed on the dairy farm, securing a long-term soil resource for the region.
1982	Shoalhaven Sand Soil and Gravel is established as a corporate entity by Tony Emery, managed by himself and his wife Maria. Tony is a fifth-generation resident of Wogamia, a 228-hectare property on the Shoalhaven River, and now the only remaining dairy upstream of Nowra.
1985	SOILCO begins composting to improve the quality of soil products.
1996	SOILCO Pty Ltd is formed as the corporate umbrella for all the business's operations. SOILCO is granted a development consent to extract, compost and manufacture soil products at Wogamia.

(Continued)

(Continued)

Year	Event
2000	Kembla Grange Distribution Centre is opened to complement the manufacturing operation in Nowra. This coincides with SOILCO extending its waste management services for Wollongong City Council north to Whytes Gully. In addition, SOILCO is awarded the Shoalhaven City Council organics processing contract.
2002	SOILCO receives an environment protection licence for composting and related activities from the NSW Environmental Protection Authority, the first company on the NSW South Coast to achieve this.
2004	SOILCO achieves product certification for composts and soil conditioners (AS4454) and landscape soils (AS4419).
2009	SOILCO receives development consent for the Kembla Grange Organics Recycling Facility and construction commences in 2010.
2012	SOILCO starts collecting commercial food waste in purpose-built collection vehicles.
2014	SOILCO is awarded the Wollongong City Council organics processing contract.
2015	SOILCO is awarded the Shellharbour City Council organics processing contract.
2016	Kembla Grange Organics Recycling Facility was upgraded to include aerated IVC technology. ISO 9001 certification is gained. In addition, SOILCO is awarded the Kiama Municipal Council organics processing contract.
2018	Wogamia composting infrastructure improvements are completed. The existing turn piled (windrow) composting infrastructure is converted to a 30,000 tonnes per annum forced aeration static pile composting system for food and garden organics. This reduces Wogamia's composting footprint from 20,000 to 5,000 m^2 and introduces better environmental and process controls.
2019	SOILCO is awarded the contract to design, build and operate an organic recycling facility for Tweed Shire Council in Northern NSW. In addition, SOILCO is awarded the City of Canterbury Bankstown organics processing contract.
2020	Kembla Grange Compost Manufacturing Facility upgrades are commenced to construct a further four IVC tunnels at an adjacent site previously used for steel pipe manufacturing.

(Continued)

Year	Event
2021	SOILCO successfully delivers an IVC facility for Tweed Shire Council. In addition, SOILCO is awarded the Ballina Shire Council organics processing contract. I Squared Capital becomes a majority shareholder in SOILCO, committing up to $300M in capital to expand SOILCO's infrastructure network. Second generation family members, Charlie and Mark Emery, retain their shareholdings and leadership positions as Managing Director and Sales and Service Manager respectively.
2022	SOILCO secures three greenfield sites for development: Badgerys Creek (Western Sydney), Pinkenba (Brisbane, Queensland) and Bromelton (Scenic Rim, Queensland).
2023	SOILCO is awarded the Cumberland City Council organics processing contract, the Blue Mountains City Council organics haulage contract and starts receiving organics for processing from Kyogle Council.
Nov 2023	SOILCO agrees to acquire Corkhill Brothers, a landscape supplies outlet and green waste recycling centre with a strong presence in Canberra and southern NSW. In addition, SOILCO officially opens its Kembla Grange Compost Manufacturing Facility (CMF). This $15 million investment will enable a major change in SOILCO's service offerings in the Illawarra, making it possible to receive, sort, screen and process an additional 40,000 tonnes of locally generated food and garden organics. SOILCO also wins a $25 million tender to design, construct and operate a new Organics Processing Facility (OPF) for Bega Valley Shire Council. This proposed purpose-built OPF, to be constructed at the council's Central Waste Facility near Wolumla, will use covered aerated static pile technology. It is expected to be completed in 2026 and will be operated independently under a 10-year contract with capacity to extend if needed.

(SOILCO, 2024d)

Clearly, SOILCO is continuing to expand its operations. In early 2024, SOILCO acquired Corkhill Bros (CBS), a family-owned and founded organisation. The acquisition has brought together two companies with similar values and more than 100 years of combined operational experience. Together, the footprint of the two organisations now extends from Southeast Queensland to southern New South Wales. The collaboration delivers a network of more than 15 sites, including greenfield developments, quarrying operations, workshops, offices and organics recycling facilities supported by distribution channels for a range of products.

Roslyn Florie-George, SOILCO's Executive General Manager – Strategic Growth and Infrastructure, is quoted by Korycki, L. (2023, para.6) on the value of the Corkhill Bros acquisition:

> As family-founded businesses with strong ties to the agricultural sector and a commitment to product quality, we've got a unique offering in the market. [...] Corkhill Brothers has a fantastic reputation in the Canberra market and has a lot to offer. By joining forces, we're able to combine Corkhill's regional experience with our in-vessel technology know-how to prepare for the next wave of source-separated organics.

Just as when I Squared gained a controlling interest in SOILCO, the Corkhill family have retained key leadership positions in the business, ensuring continuity. The acquisition and recent contract wins have not disrupted either company's existing services or contracts. Philip Corkhill, Managing Director of CBS, said in a joint statement with SOILCO (Korycki, 2023, para.10):

> [...] joining forces with SOILCO will make it possible to tap into a broader pool of resources, knowledge, and experience to benefit customers and the environment. Together we will be able to achieve greater efficiencies and deliver the organics infrastructure needed to meet ambitious resource recovery targets.

The Impact of Family

While researching this case, the author asked Charlie whether he felt that SOILCO was still a family business and what effect, if any, its family origins had on SOILCO's commitment to the goals of SDG#15. Charlie had to think about it. After all, since late 2021 I Squared has held a majority interest in SOILCO, an obvious contrast to the traditional ownership and management transfer from older to younger generation which typifies many family businesses. Charlie and Mark Emery together hold the remaining interest; no other family members are directly involved. I Squared keeps a close eye on the performance of the business and Charlie and Mark, as SOILCO's leaders, report to I Squared about this regularly.

On the other hand, as Charlie points out, SOILCO originated from the passion of the founder, Tony Emery, in giving life to soil and Tony had imparted this passion to him and Mark. As Charlie recalls it, around 2020 Tony had said to him and Mark that the business would need major capital investment if it were to maintain its place in the market. Maria and Tony did not want to take on further debt – in fact they wanted to retire. The family had lived on the land where the dairy farm was located for five generations, but they had never actually owned it. So, if Charlie and Mark wanted the business to continue 'they would need to put their money where their mouth is.'

The partnership with I Squared has helped Charlie and Mark 'see Tony and Maria secure and settled': that is, debt-free and enjoying the retirement they sought. Charlie said his parents now have a shack at the beach where Tony at last truly relaxes:

> If he (Tony) was here he would be on site all the time, still working in the business. (C. Emery, personal communication, June 14, 2024)

In this way, some of the classic problems of generational transfer in family firms have been faced and overcome perhaps more so than in conventionally structured family businesses. Moreover, as is typical in family businesses, members of the second generation are keen to maintain and expand the vision of the founders. As Charlie put it in the announcement of I Squared Capital's investment:

> SOILCO founders Tony and Ria Emery have provided a fantastic platform for Mark and I. We feel this is a perfect way to cap off their personal business journey and the entire SOILCO team are enormously grateful to be able to continue to deliver their vision to improve Australian soils and regenerate our environment for dynamic growth. (SOILCO, 2021, para.4)

In adopting and developing SOILCO's mission to 'give life to soil', Charlie sees a clear point of difference between SOILCO and other waste management firms which are focused primarily on collection and disposal of waste, albeit in responsible ways. As he sees it, because those firms do not make use of sophisticated scientific and technological developments the way SOILCO does, they cannot take up the SDG#15 challenge of rehabilitating soil and transforming degraded land to a standard which meets the needs of the communities that live on or near that land. Charlie Emery's commitment to those goals is reflected in the fact that he is a director and national chair of the Australian Organics Recycling Association and chair of that organisation's NSW committee.

Another characteristic of the business that recalls its family origins is that SOILCO develops its staff. Charlie points out that the employee who does all SOILCO's SCADA (data visualisation) work had come to SOILCO straight from high school. His first job with SOILCO was driving a front-end loader. Employees say SOILCO *feels* like a family business. Its focus is on achievement: people are encouraged to do their best work and develop career skills. SOILCO is focused on maintaining a family business feel.

Charlie recalls that his mother, Maria Emery, had been the person who pushed others in the business to take advantage of training and other services offered by Family Business Australia (FBA), the peak body for family businesses in

Australia and New Zealand.[2] She persuaded members of SOILCO to use family business advisors and to adopt appropriate governance structures as the firm grew. Now, with more than 140 staff, SOILCO has middle management structures that allow efficient sharing of knowledge and create a career path for staff to reach higher levels. Charlie is still a member of an FBA forum group (a group whose members share business problems on a confidential basis and learn from each other).

Most of all, Charlie says, SOILCO is a family-*led* business. I Squared Capital looks to SOILCO to create and justify its goals and strategies and it keeps a close eye on how well the strategies are working. But SOILCO management still creates the strategies and, as Charlie says, 'it is still our name on the door'.

The partnership with I Squared Capital, a private equity firm focusing on global infrastructure investments, also reinforces SOILCO's original family business values. I Squared invests its members' superannuation and other funds in energy, utilities, transport and telecom projects in North America, Europe and select high growth economies, such as India and China. The projects must be consistent with I Squared's ethical investment focus. I Squared approached SOILCO because it was attracted to SOILCO's ethical approach which, as noted earlier, is influenced by its family roots and values. I Squared saw their investment in SOILCO as:

> [...] the first step in building a state-of-the-art waste processing and recycling platform in Australia, which we believe will benefit from our global experience of building some of the leading companies across green and sustainable infrastructure in the water and waste management, renewable energy, and energy transition sectors. (SOILCO, 2021, para.3)

SDG#15 Life on Land and SOILCO

SOILCO's products and services address not just life *ON* land, but the life *OF* land. Its vision and mission which originated with Tony Emery considerably predate the UN Sustainable Development Goals (SDGs). In other words, SOILCO was dealing with the needs of the soil and figuring out how to sustain it before this became a global preoccupation. SOILCO's mission speaks to the first five of the SDG#15 Targets, namely:

(1) SDG#15.1, which is to conserve and restore terrestrial and freshwater ecosystems;
(2) SDG#15.2 which is to end deforestation and restore degraded forests;
(3) SDG#15.3 which aims to end desertification and restore degraded land;
(4) SDG#15.4 which aims to ensure conservation of mountain ecosystems and
(5) SDG#15.5 which aims to protect biodiversity and natural habitats.

---

[2]Now named Family Business Association.

In addition, regarding SDG#15.8, *prevent* invasive alien species *on land and in water ecosystems*, SOILCO must meet stringent legal requirements for the safety of its products and also observe safety regulations for staff operating equipment, handling product, moving product to different parts of Australia and so on. Again, this speaks to the complexity of running a business like SOILCO. As Charlie explains:

> People have seen that we've made a strong start with recycling food waste. So, they're always saying to me, 'I guess this means you'll be doing food waste recycling everywhere now.' Not at all. We can't just set up food recycling everywhere. Everything depends on the link between the particular SOILCO location and the nearby community. There's a difference between what we can do when residential properties are located five kilometres away and when they're 50 kilometres away. (C. Emery, personal communication, 14 June, 2024)

SOILCO actively promotes the circular economy to manage climate change. As explained in the videos on SOILCO's website, any CO_2 which can be replaced in the earth is a move in the direction of managing climate change, that is, restoring the balance between fossil layer carbon removed and replaced.

Because SOILCO has worked towards SDG#15 goals for so long, it often finds itself advising local, state and federal government bodies on actions to promote environmental sustainability. This addresses SDG#15.9: *integrate ecosystem and biodiversity in governmental planning*. As with all its clients, SOILCO works collaboratively with government bodies to help them understand how their needs are best met by understanding the issues in their immediate environment. This increases awareness and understanding of what everyone can do to live more sustainably and provides some hope in the battle to manage climate change which, for most people, appears only as a bad news story.

The Future for SOILCO and SDG#15

Backed by their funding partner I Squared and with the knowledge that they are extending the insights and legacy of SOILCO's founders, Tony and Maria Emery, Charlie and Mark Emery, their middle management staff, and a small army of manufacturing, driving and other staff, are well placed to tackle the future including pursuing the goals of SDG#15. In the immediate term, SOILCO will be busy developing the three greenfield sites they secured in 2022 and 2023 into large-scale organics recovery facilities.

Fig. 7.2 shows Charlie and Mark Emery, second-generation business leaders from the Emery family, and the SOILCO logo. The logo was originally created to reflect the soil and the natural environment, with the Shoalhaven river flowing through the centre. Although the logo has been modernised in recent years, these original design features have been retained and pay tribute to the family farm and

Fig. 7.2.   Charlie Emery (Left) and Mark Emery (Right). *Source:* SOILCO (2024e).

location of SOILCO's first composting facility, which continues to operate today. It reminds us that land and water resources will increasingly demand our care. The way ahead is not straight, but it is not too tortuous either. The destination is not visible: sustaining the environment is an ongoing task.

References

Korycki, L. (2023, December 7). SOILCO expands footprint with Corkhill Bros acquisition. *Waste Management Review*. https://wastemanagementreview.com.au/soilco-expands-footprint-with-corkhill-bros-acquisition/

SOILCO. (2021). Company annoncement SOILCO and I squared capital. https://soilco.com.au/company-announcement-soilco-and-i-squared-capital/

SOILCO. (2024a). About us. *SOILCO*. https://soilco.com.au/our-company/

SOILCO. (2024b). Mission & vision. https://soilco.com.au/our-company/mission-vision/

SOILCO. (2024c). Philosophy. https://soilco.com.au/our-company/philosophy/

SOILCO. (2024d). News: Clean energy compost manufacturing facility proposed for Badgerys Creek. https://soilco.com.au/clean-energy-compost-manufacturing-facility-proposed-for-badgerys-creek/

SOILCO. (2024e). SOILCO expands footprint with Corkhill Bros acquisition. https://soilco.com.au/soilco-expands-footprint-with-corkhill-bros-acquisition/

United Nations. (n.d.). Goals: 15. *United Nations*. https://sdgs.un.org/goals/goal15#targets_and_indicators

Chapter 8

UAE: MyHive Enterprise Advancing SDG 15 With Sustainable Beekeeping and Biodiversity

Jacinta Dsilva

SEE Institute, The Sustainable City, Dubai, UAE

Introduction

Biodiversity is necessary for human well-being and survival. Pollinators such as bees are crucial for most of our crop production, providing foods like fruits and herbs. Soil health relies on invertebrates and microbes, which support plant growth. There are several other examples of how biodiversity supports humankind. For example, trees clean the air and absorb carbon dioxide, acting as an immense supporter in climate change management. Coastal ecosystems like coral reefs and mangroves protect against erosion and storms. Nature also helps humans in improving our physical and mental health just by spending time in nature, and with urban green spaces reducing stress and lowering blood pressure it would be a challenging endeavour if we did not have nature's support. Thus, preserving biodiversity is vital for food security, health and environmental stability (Royal Society, 2024).

Bees are more than just small insects collecting honey. They are critical for biodiversity and health across the world. They provide high-quality food such as honey, royal jelly, pollen and other products such as beeswax, propolis and honeybee venom. Over 90% of the top 107 crops globally are pollinated by bees, although wind- and self-pollinated grasses, which do not depend on animal pollination, make up approximately 60% of the world's food production (Patel et al., 2020). Let's look at some of the benefits of having bees on this planet; the most known function of bees is their role as pollinators. Bees contribute to food production. According to the United Nations Food and Agriculture Organisation, three out of four fruit or seed production depends on pollinators such as bees (Ritchie, 2021). Economically, bees contribute to the livelihood of people by providing products such as honey, bee venom and royal jelly. Bees also play an important role in the maintenance of biodiversity by transporting pollen from flower to flower and fertilising a huge variety of plants and trees.

Attaining the 2030 Sustainable Development Goal of Life on Land, 97–107
Copyright © 2025 Jacinta Dsilva
Published under exclusive licence by Emerald Publishing Limited
doi:10.1108/978-1-83608-212-520241008

There are more than 20,000 known bee species, with new species still being discovered. However, bee populations have been declining at an alarming rate due to various environmental factors (MacInnis et al., 2023). Globally the demand for food has been soaring due to population explosion, which pushes agricultural practices to become more extensive for an increased crop yield, which damages ecosystems and reduces biodiversity while increasing greenhouse gas emissions, which is a huge negative externality. Due to urbanisation and globalisation, our cities are expanding, leading to a drastic change in land use that negatively impacts the habitat of bees and other creatures. Additionally, climate change contributes to all sorts of changes such as rising global temperatures, change in weather patterns leading to significant stress to bee populations.

Beekeeping or apiculture is a non-agricultural activity that involves the practical management of social species of bees to produce food and agriculture. It is highly complementary to agricultural and horticultural production. Alaa Mustafa the CEO of MyHive in the UAE was not aware of the impact nor the benefits of bees. He was introduced to beekeeping by his brother Faris Saeed, who is the Chairman and CEO of SEE Holding and Founder of The Sustainable City, Dubai.

On 20 May 2018, World Bee Day, Faris Saeed and Alaa Mustafa launched MyHive in collaboration with Alaska Native Health Board in the Sustainable City and asked Alaa to manage it. MyHive is dedicated to ensuring that the local community receives the best honey whilst also enabling those who take interest in Beekeeping to partake in educational material or in a more interactive method (visiting the beehives), thus satisfying SDG#15.

Services Offered by MyHive

Adopt a Hive – Individuals can adopt a beehive, in which the MyHive team will maintain it for the bee parents. Subscribers will receive naturally produced honey from their beehives.

Honey Production – producing local honey in three seasons using Sidr trees in October and November, Samar trees in May and June and Ghaf trees in June and July.

Beekeeping workshops – workshops on bee health, beekeeping for beginners at The Sustainable City, Dubai to educate children and adults about the importance of the role of bees as pollinators of food and how to take care of the hives.

The Vision and Mission Statement of MyHive

MyHive's mission is to promote the vital role of bees within the ecological system while sharing the wonders of sustainable honey production practices. It also intends to focus on providing education about sustainable beekeeping, protecting and promoting bees through the adoption of beehives and advocating for sustainable and ethical beekeeping practices.

Background – MyHive Social Enterprise

Alaa Mustafa was first introduced to the beekeeping world in 2018 through his brother, Faris Saeed, who encouraged him to embark on establishing a sustainable initiative that revolved around beekeeping. Faris was interested in spearheading a net zero emissions future through redefining infrastructure and cities by developing sustainable cities and communities, particularly, after the financial crisis of 2008. Therefore, Faris and his partner Wassim, who were popular developers and had constructed several residential and commercial towers in the UAE in the past, realised that the traditional way of conducting business will not work in the present condition since they were aware that built environment sector contributes to around 40% of carbon emissions; therefore, they started thinking how to create a model for sustainable real estate. That's when they invested time in understanding sustainability in a comprehensive manner by visiting different countries where such a model was already successful. They realised that most communities were focusing on just one of the aspects of sustainability, that's when they understood that to make a project sustainable, they must combine the three pillars of sustainability. According to Faris Saeed, '*to make a project sustainable you have to combine the three elements – environment, society and economics – together*' (Developers, 2019). And the idea of the first sustainable city in the UAE was born in 2014.

The construction began in 2015 and the first residents moved in at the end of 2016 into the first fully operational environmentally friendly community in the Middle East by Diamond Developers called 'The Sustainable City' (TSC). The city integrated local species in its landscapes and created a suitable natural environment for bees, bats, butterflies and birds while the urban farm and green spine provide ample natural spaces for outdoor fun and educational activities. TSC demonstrates a comprehensive approach to sustainability, integrating environmental, social and economic pillars to create a thriving, eco-friendly community. This city stands out with its ambitious efforts to support biodiversity, underscoring the importance of ecological balance within urban development. Environmentally, the city incorporates green building practices, renewable energy sources and extensive recycling programs, significantly reducing its carbon footprint. A key feature is its extensive green spaces, which include biodiverse farms, community gardens and indigenous plant species that enhance local flora and fauna. These efforts not only beautify the city but also create habitats for various species, promoting ecological resilience.

Socially, the Sustainable City fosters a strong sense of community and environmental stewardship among its residents. Educational programs and community activities emphasise the importance of sustainability and biodiversity, encouraging residents to actively participate in conservation efforts. The city's design promotes walkability and reduces reliance on vehicles, thereby enhancing air quality and residents' well-being. Economically, the city exhibits that sustainable practices can be cost-effective. By implementing energy-efficient systems and waste reduction strategies, the city lowers operational costs while creating green jobs. This economic model supports long-term growth and stability, showcasing how sustainability can drive economic benefits.

To further promote sustainable living, TSC launched a community-wide biodiversity assessment programme. It deployed monitoring equipment to measure the impact of urban ecology on biodiversity and ecosystem health. The Sustainable City was the region's first community to monitor and measure the health of its ecosystem, in association with Emirates Nature-WWF, by installing advanced monitoring equipment, like ultrasound recorders for bats and audio recorders for birds; to monitor the diversity of local species (Home-3 – The Sustainable City, 2024).

On World Bee Day, May 2018, Faris Saeed and Alaa Mustafa launched MyHive in the Sustainable City Dubai, in collaboration with Alaska Native Health Board. Faris asked his brother Alaa to manage it completely since Faris wanted to focus on increasing the positive impact on the built environment sector by developing more sustainable cities and communities. Alaa expressed his weariness of the beekeeping at first, admitting '*It was a bit weird at first but now I love it, because it is different*' (A. Mustafa, personal communication, 21 June 2024). After in depth research, Alaa grew to love and appreciate the niche business of beekeeping and started managing MyHive with other family members. It was also supported by a member of the Ras Al Khaimah government who liked the concept, but they decided to part ways after some time. The concept was to give customers the ability to 'Adopt a Beehive' and get to enjoy the delicious and naturally produced honey from their beehives. MyHive started seeing significant involvement from TSC residents. Approximately, 10 residents adopted beehives during the inaugural year of MyHive, with one enthusiastic member even ordering 10 hives.

Initially, the hives were kept in the sustainable city, but as the number of hives started growing, they had to find a better place to accommodate honeybees for the safety of the bees and the residents; therefore Alaa shifted the hives in remote areas such as Ras Al Khaimah, since the weather is a bit more conducive for the bees to survive compared to the Dubai climate. A sizeable number of TSC residents are the members of the hives and enjoy 10 kilograms of honey every year. Alaa mentioned

> One member took 10 hives, and we supplied him with 50 kg of honey so that he can give it to his close and extended family. Some people even take the bee wax during the cedar time and eat it. It feels like chewing gum. (A. Mustafa, personal communication, 21 June 2024).

Once beekeeping had fully grabbed Alaa's attention, he began devoting much of his time to reading, studying and visiting other beekeeping farms to learn best practices of maintaining beehives. His research allowed him to learn a plethora of information, including the benefits of local honey compared to imported honey. He described how local honey is produced with all the protective benefits regarding our environment. The honey produced in the UAE provides health benefits to those who live in the UAE with its arid, blisteringly hot and dry climate. Similarly, the honey produced by bees in Canada would provide health benefits to those living in the cold and dry temperatures of Canada. Ultimately, MyHive is working towards SDG#15 by protecting and promoting humanity's relationship with bees, specifically in the UAE, and by utilising sustainable beekeeping practices and harvesting honey in a sustainable manner.

All the above practices are managed by taking Monofloral honey directly from the beehives, collected by the honeybees from local areas (Abu Dhabi, Hatta Dubai and Fujairah) and is 100% natural. The honey is then packed under sterile conditions without the use of heating or filtration.

SDG #15 Life on Land and MyHive

The purpose of MyHive is to educate the people of the UAE on sustainable beekeeping, the protection of indigenous bees and to provide free educational support to the public about beekeeping along with producing natural honey through sustainable beekeeping practices. Their mission aligns very well with SDG# 15 of Life on Land by protecting and promoting terrestrial ecosystems. An example of this would be MyHive facilitating the adoption of beehives for their subscribers to protect and multiply the bee population in the UAE and taking on high maintenance task of managing beehives for bee lovers satisfying SDG#15.1 and SDG#15.2 SDG targets, which pertains to the conservation, restoration, and sustainable use of terrestrial ecosystems, as well as sustainable management.

SDG#15.5, which refers to action being taken to reduce the degradation of natural habitats by protecting the bees from dying due to extreme heat conditions and allowing the local community to be involved in protecting the environment, is also being achieved by MyHive.

MyHive further satisfies SDG#15.6, which refers to the 'fair and equitable sharing of the benefits arising from the utilisation of genetic resources and promote appropriate access to such resources', and SDG#4 i.e. by providing free education by offering interactive apiary visits at least twice a year as well as the opportunity for beekeeping enthusiasts to attend beekeeping workshops to maintain a beehive of their own.

According to Alaa, most honey producers and beekeepers perform beekeeping for commercial purposes, i.e. once the honey harvesting is completed, they generally let the bees die since there are several challenges of managing the bees and some of the traders cannot afford to manage them (Randy, 2012). MyHive is notably different with their sustainable approach to beekeeping since they do not let their bees die after the harvest season is over, but take on the burden of maintaining the beehives in two ways; during the seasons where honey cannot be produced, MyHive shifts the bees from farm to farm to protect them from heat as well to provide them with food (either the honey they've produced or other organic food such as watermelon). During the start of the season the hives are cleaned by Alaa's employees (they have hired 10 contract employees who are specialists in beekeeping) to maintain the hygiene of the bees and the quality of honey. Alaa also mentioned that some beekeepers even feed refined sugar (sucrose) to bees as food however that just increases the nutritional deficiency among the bees and could also damage their digestive processes leading to poor quality of royal jelly and eventually poor quality of honey (Bee Seasonal, 2018).

The UAE is committed to conserving its desert environment and terrestrial ecosystems as part of its heritage. Federal Law No. 24 of 1999 aims to protect and enhance the environment, develop natural resources, conserve biodiversity and promote sustainable usage across the country. In 2013, the UAE introduced a four-year national strategy and action plan for biosecurity to protect against biological hazards. A key aspect of the UAE's environmental policies is raising awareness among the younger generation to encourage responsible behaviour towards natural resources. This effort is supported by 'The National Environmental Education and Awareness Strategy 2015–2021', which aligns with international standards and stakeholder expectations. The strategy focuses on educating UAE youth for a sustainable future and strengthening the community's commitment to sustainability and environmental protection. MyHive and the bee parents are working tirelessly to align with the UAE laws to protect the biodiversity of the country and create awareness among different age groups and nationalities about protecting nature and endangered species such as wild bees. These actions are seeking to achieve SDG#15.5 in the protection of biodiversity and natural habitats.

To maintain the safety of the honey at MyHive, once the honey is removed from the hives, samples are sent to labs for testing the purity of the honey and only then they are filled in the jars to be given to their subscribers and to be sold otherwise. Now, MyHive also has a retail store where 100% natural honey is available for anyone to buy for personal use and gifting purposes. For example, The SEE Institute, located in the Sustainable City, purchases MyHive honey to give as corporate gifts.

A Business Model and SDG #15 Life on Land

The business model of MyHive is based on two central pillars: Educate the general public about beekeeping and the conservation of indigenous bee species while harvesting honey using sustainable practices.

To ensure that SDG#15 can be fulfilled, the following objectives are internalised by the members of MyHive:

- To promote the excellence of UAE honey to the global market.
- To educate the UAE public on:

  - The importance of the honeybee for the UAE and the global ecosystem.
  - The importance of the honeybee as vital pollinators for UAE flora and commercial farmers.
  - The benefits of honey as a natural food source.
- To promote sustainable beekeeping best practices within the UAE.

SDG#15 Life on Land and the Stakeholders of MyHive

A business, irrespective of a profit or non-profit making entity, cannot thrive without the foundation or support of good stakeholders. Their role is crucial in making wise decisions in the functioning of an organisation. When discussing SDG#15, stakeholders play a significant role in achieving the goals in several ways. For example, they can support the decision of protecting certain types of local flora and fauna as well as encourage the organisation to plant more native flowering plants and trees that create a better ecosystem.

At MyHive, the stakeholders, particularly TSC management and the residents, have been very active in contributing to achieving SDG#15 by engaging in a range of impactful activities. First, by promoting biodiversity through sustainable beekeeping practices and supporting local flora and fauna and encouraging the planting of native flowering plants and trees in the local communities in the UAE. The most expensive honey is from the Sidr Tree, as Alaa mentions,

> The blossom from the Sidr tree provides rich food for bees to produce honey in October and November. This honey is the most expensive, but tastiest type of honey. From May to June, Samar honey is produced (Samar is local tree found in the UAE), which contains healing properties, and lastly Ghaf honey (Ghaf is local drought tolerant tree found in the UAE), characterised by its reddish tint is produced during June and July. (A. Mustafa, personal communication, 21 June 2024)

This leads to Alaa and his team taking the bees from one Emirate to the other as the individual seasons approach.

Research and innovation also play a crucial role. Supporting scientific research on bee health, biodiversity and sustainable agriculture and collaborating with academic institutions to study the impacts of beekeeping on local ecosystems can lead to the development of innovative solutions that enhance sustainability. Alaa has been researching sustainable beekeeping from the time he took on the CEO role. He mentioned some fascinating details about beekeeping that he learnt, such as the dangers of moving a beehive during the daytime as during daytime, bees are going out in search of honey, and if the beehive is moved, the bees that ventured out will be unable to find their hive, thus resulting in bees becoming agitated and stinging people versus if the hive is shifted during the nighttime, all the members of the beehive will be in one when morning comes, the bees will navigate using their memory to carry out their routine.

Sustainable business practices, such as ethical production of honey, producing eco-friendly bee products, supporting local beekeepers and encouraging sustainable livelihoods is an important role MyHive is working on. Initially, Alaa received great support from the Sustainable city residents and with word of mouth spreading across the region they have had subscribers for as long as 10 years. When the project was introduced to the TSC residents, they were quite intrigued by the idea of having beehives in their backyard and in the community. They worked closely with MyHive to engage in different activities such as beekeeping workshops. Several residents became bee parents and have been supporting the initiative for many years.

The business model of MyHive is very simple, as it runs on a subscription model; those who are interested in becoming bee parents must complete a basic form and pay the subscription fee of AED750 + vat charges and people can adopt a hive for three years. During the first season, i.e. the Sidr, the subscriber pays AED787.50 (inclusive of vat), the next instalment is during the Samar season and the last one is Ghaf season during July, in total the subscribers receive 10 kgs equivalent to 20 jars of 500 grams per jar for a total of AED3,150 in the first year and AED2,363 for the second and the third year of subscription. Each of the honey types has a different taste and are used for several medical purposes; however, Samar honey is particularly special as it is the best alternative for sugar. The subscribers enjoy the tastiest honey at a much lower cost compared to regular store prices with the assurance that it was ethically produced. The subscribers also can visit the apiary (farm) once or twice in a year during the seasonal period. Currently, MyHive manages approximately 189 hives for its subscribers. Alaa mentioned that 'we do not make major profits therefore our return on investment is not monetary but relates to how MyHive helps and supports the bee population in the UAE' (A. Mustafa, personal communication, 21 June 2024).

After much effort, MyHive started receiving some recognition from the UAE government for example in 2019 their effort was recognised by Abu Dhabi Agriculture and Food Safety Authority for their contribution to innovation in agriculture (see Fig. 8.1). They also received an award as 'Best Honeycomb' by ApiArab Expo, Abu Dhabi National Exhibition Centre in 2019 (see Fig. 8.2).

However, when the COVID pandemic hit, it was very challenging for MyHive to survive since the entire UAE was in lockdown and taking hives from one place to another was a major challenge, so Alaa and his team collaborated with local beekeepers and they maintained the hives for MyHive; therefore, the bees could

هيئة أبوظبي للزراعة والسلامة الغذائية
ABU DHABI AGRICULTURE AND FOOD
SAFETY AUTHORITY

Certificate of Appreciation

Abu Dhabi Agriculture and Food Safety Authority is honored to award this certificate to

MY HIVE INITIATIVE-THE SUSTAINABLE CITY

In recognition of your contribution to the success of the Global Forum for Innovations in Agriculture

Abu Dhabi National Exhibition Center, Abu Dhabi, United Arab Emirates, 1-2 April 2019

Thank You for Participating

Eng. Thamer Rashed Al Qasemi
Chairman of GFIA Organizing Committee

Fig. 8.1.   Certificate of Appreciation by MyHive.

Fig. 8.2.   Best Honeycomb Award in 2019.

survive the pandemic and the subscribers could get their share of honey. They tried their best to keep the bees alive through various means, but some of the bees passed away due to limited food and other related reasons. Before COVID, they had more than 1,000 hives however due the death of the bees they remained with around 500 hives. But after the lockdown was over Alaa made sure that all the bees received extra care and support to survive and produce good quality honey.

Reporting and Measurement

MyHive efforts can be measured in several ways such as the regular measurements and observations taking place of the bee population as well as the appraisal of the variety of trees that support pollinators. They can also track the number of habitats as well as the quantity of honey produced. Since they are a small team and lack the expertise in implementing any specific method of metrics or narratives to evaluate or measure the impact of business they are working closely with The Sustainable City and the SEE Institute to develop some strong mechanisms to get more data and measure the impact in the future. Alaa also mentioned that they train their direct and third-party employees in maintaining records of the time they take the bees from one place to another, and the behaviour changes of the bees is another area where Alaa focuses quite often.

Challenges of Working with SDG#15

When Alaa was asked about the challenges, he mentioned the environment, especially the blistering heat of the UAE, which is a major challenge as the blistering heat causes huge losses in the bee population. Therefore, making it difficult for MyHive to maintain the beehives. Another challenge is monitoring the bees when they are out of their hives collecting honey from the pollen. Due to the negative impact of chemicals that are sprayed on plants and trees, bees are bound to bring bad substances back to the hive, jeopardising the quality of honey. But as Alaa says, *bees are very sensitive*, if they notice that one of the bees have brought in a bad substance, the other bees do not allow that contaminated bee to lay the pollen in the hive and they build a mechanism that kills that specific bee. Therefore, monitoring the bees is a crucial task and the team works diligently to make sure that the honey produced in the hives is of a good quality and does not harm anyone.

What Next for MyHive and SDG# 15

Overall, Alaa Mustafa and Faris Saeed have demonstrated an ambition and leadership through MyHive and The Sustainable City, Dubai that have persevered despite challenges such as a high maintenance cost and the arid climate of the UAE. Alaa constantly seeks knowledge, whether it be from books, YouTube or visiting other bee farms and talking to people. Alaa's persistence proved successful as he gained the attention of the UAE government and was recognised for the initiative in 2019. Alaa also tries to find other beekeepers with a similar concept, but he has not found any who do it for passion. He believes that their business has a purpose to protect bees and to produce honey using sustainable practices that support local requirements while being environmentally conscious. Going forward, Alaa wants to create a platform to educate others on beekeeping since he believes that education can add value to youth and urban beekeepers in the UAE. He believes that there is so much to do and wants to grow it to its full potential in the UAE and find people or authorities who will empower the enterprise further.

In conclusion, MyHive and The Sustainable City, Dubai can execute an operational model that strives to embody a harmony between the environment and humanity by preserving the environment and its terrestrial ecosystem. MyHive has protected and multiplied the population of bees as well as harvest honey using sustainable practices and generated educational content for subscribers to both understand and act upon the idea of safekeeping the environment, its organisms and the wonder of biodiversity through their beekeeping activities. The Sustainable City, Dubai fosters an environment where environmental protection and its heterogeneity is safeguarded in a sustainable way and promotes a circular economic way of life.

References

Bee Seasonal. (2018). *Bees should eat HONEY!* Bee Seasonal. https://beeseasonal.com/blogs/every-honey-tells-a-story/artificially-feeding-bees-is-a-bad-idea-sustainable-honey-brands

Developers, D. (2019, June 30). *Faris Saeed: The man who built utopia – The Sustainable City*. The Sustainable City. https://www.thesustainablecity.ae/2019/06/30/faris-saeed-the-man-who-built-utopia/. Accessed on July 22, 2024.

Home-3 – The Sustainable City. (2024, March 19). The Sustainable City. https://thesustainablecity.com/. Accessed on July 22, 2024.

MacInnis, G., Normandin, E., & Ziter, C. D. (2023). Decline in wild bee species richness associated with honeybee (*Apis mellifera* L.) abundance in an urban ecosystem. *PeerJ, 11*, e14699. https://doi.org/10.7717/peerj.14699

Patel, V., Pauli, N., Biggs, E., Barbour, L., & Boruff, B. (2020). Why bees are critical for achieving sustainable development. *Ambio, 50*(1), 49–59. https://doi.org/10.1007/s13280-020-01333-9

Randy, O. (2012, February 24). *The "Rules" for successful beekeeping – Scientific Beekeeping*. Scientific Beekeeping. https://scientificbeekeeping.com/the-rules-for-successful-beekeeping/

Ritchie, H. (2021). *How much of the world's food production is dependent on pollinators?* Our World in Data. https://ourworldindata.org/pollinator-dependence

Royal Society. (2024). *Why is biodiversity important?* Royal Society. https://royalsociety.org/news-resources/projects/biodiversity/why-is-biodiversity-important/

Chapter 9

Chile: Emiliana Vineyard – Family Businesses in the Wine Sector and Sustainability

Claudio G. Muller

Texas Tech University, USA

Introduction

Chile, with its unique geographical conditions, has emerged as a formidable player in the global wine market. Nestled between the Andes Mountains, the Pacific Ocean, the Atacama Desert and Patagonia, Chile's sunny weather, thermal amplitude, and soil quality create an ideal environment for vineyards. However, Chile ranks only 28th out of 193 countries in the Sustainable Development Report Index (Sachs et al., 2020), which places the country in an unfavourable position of competitiveness that hints at the absence of long-term sustainable policies.

Emiliana Vineyard, owned and managed by the Guilisasti Family, stands as a beacon of sustainable wine production in Chile. The family's leadership and their ownership of the number one wine-producing company in Chile, Concha y Toro Vineyard, have been instrumental in promoting sustainable practices in the industry.

Chile and the Wine Sector

Chile is one of the world's leading wine-producing countries, renowned for its diverse climates which is ideal for viticulture. The country's wine industry is characterised by an arid desert in the north, the Atacama and cold and rainy regions in the south. Chile's varied geography offers a wide range of conditions suitable for different grape varieties, allowing for the production of a wide spectrum of wine styles.

Chilean wines have gained international recognition for their quality and value. The country stands out mainly for its Cabernet Sauvignon, Carmenere and Sauvignon Blanc, among other varieties. One of the competitive advantages of the

Attaining the 2030 Sustainable Development Goal of Life on Land, 109–117
Copyright © 2025 Claudio G. Muller
Published under exclusive licence by Emerald Publishing Limited
doi:10.1108/978-1-83608-212-520241009

Chilean wine industry is that it has quickly adopted modern viticulture and winemaking techniques. Government programs have encouraged the development of local technology and the University–Industry–Government alliance (known as Triple Helix). This has meant that wine production processes have combined traditional methods with state-of-the-art technology to improve wine quality and production efficiency (Basso et al., 2024).

On the other hand, the Chilean wine sector has experienced significant growth in recent decades, becoming a major player in the global wine market. The focus has been on the export market, where Chile is one of the leading wine-exporting countries, with important markets such as the United States, China, the United Kingdom and Brazil.

Some Examples of Organic Transition Initiatives

Chile's wine industry has been at the forefront of adopting organic and sustainable practices. The country's natural environment, with its dry climate and minimal pest pressure, is particularly conducive to organic viticulture. Some of these initiatives have been aligned with the fact that many Chilean wineries have sought organic certification, adhering to strict standards prohibiting synthetic chemicals and GMOs. Certification bodies such as the Institute for Marketecology (IMO) and USDA Organic ensure compliance with organic farming practices. Other practices have been biodynamic farming; some wineries have gone beyond organic practices to embrace biodynamic farming, which includes holistic and ecological approaches to vineyard management. This method involves composting, planting according to lunar cycles and improving biodiversity (Muhie, 2023).

As in other regions, water management and its efficient use have been fundamental in many wine regions of Chile. Wineries are implementing advanced irrigation, rainwater harvesting and water recycling techniques to conserve this vital resource (Charlin et al., 2023). One of the leading Organic Wineries in Chile is Viña Emiliana. As we mentioned, Emiliana is a leader in organic and biodynamic viticulture, producing high-quality wines that prioritise environmental sustainability. Other actors are Cono Sur and Viña Koyle, located in the Colchagua Valley.

These practices have not only had a profound impact on the Chilean wine industry but also on the environment. A report indicates that by 2022, more than 15 vineyards out of 200 already have sustainable practices, partly following Emiliana's good practices, paving the way for a more sustainable future for the wine industry (Vinos de Chile Annual Mémoire, 2023). One effect that these wineries have achieved is that Chilean wines are increasingly recognised not only for their quality but also for their environmental credentials, a testament to Chile's commitment to sustainable wine production. This has enhanced the country's reputation in the global wine market, filling Chileans with pride for their contribution to sustainability.

On the other hand, growing consumer awareness and demand for organic and sustainable products have prompted more wineries in other regions, such as Argentina, to adopt these practices, ensuring they remain competitive and meet market expectations. The Chilean wine sector is a dynamic and innovative industry committed to quality and sustainability. Many wineries' widespread adoption of organic and sustainable practices highlights Chile's role as a leader in environmentally responsible wine production (Cederberg et al., 2008). As the global demand for sustainable products grows, Chile's wine industry is well-positioned to meet these demands while protecting and enhancing its unique wine heritage (Müller & Randolph, 2024).

The Guilisasti Family

The Guilisasti family is among the most influential and respected families in the Chilean wine industry. They have been at the forefront of promoting sustainable viticulture and producing high-quality wines that have gained international recognition. Their contributions span several generations and have played a pivotal role in transforming and modernising the Chilean wine sector (Lluch, 2008).

The Guilisasti family's involvement in the wine industry began with Don Melchor de Concha y Toro's founding of Viña Concha y Toro at the end of the 19th century (Concha y Toro, 2024a). The family's entrepreneurial spirit and vision laid the foundation for what would become one of Chile's largest and most prestigious wineries.

Under the leadership of the Guilisasti family, Viña Concha y Toro expanded significantly, becoming one of the world's leading wine producers. Concha y Toro has successfully penetrated international markets, consolidating itself as an essential exporter of Chilean wines. Its brands, such as Casillero del Diablo, are recognised worldwide (Concha y Toro, 2024a).

However, the Guilisasti family's most notable contribution to sustainable viticulture is through the ownership and management of Viña Emiliana, which has become a benchmark for organic and biodynamic wine production in Chile (Emiliana, 2024b).

Family involvement has been remarkable. The second generation is currently in charge and is the one that has given the company an international boost. Some family members are Rafael Guilisasti who has held several leadership positions at Viña Concha y Toro (Lluch, 2008). Rafael has strongly advocated for sustainability in the wine industry, promoting practices that enhance environmental and social responsibility. Another outstanding member is José Guilisasti, Chile's Father of Organic Viticulture (Emiliana, 2024a). José was crucial in Emiliana's transition to organic and biodynamic farming. His commitment and dedication were instrumental in establishing Emiliana as a leader in sustainable wine production. Although José passed away in 2014, his legacy continues to influence the winery's operations and commitment to sustainability. Other prominent family members include Isabel Guilisasti, who has been involved in marketing and brand development at Concha y Toro, helping to elevate the winery's global presence and reputation (Concha y Toro, 2024b). A younger member but with great participation in family decisions is Eduardo Guilisasti, who has acted as CEO of Viña Concha y Toro. Eduardo has overseen significant growth and expansion, reinforcing the winery's commitment to quality and innovation.

Through Viña Emiliana, the Guilisasti family has set a high standard for organic and sustainable viticulture, inspiring other wineries to adopt similar practices (Cain, 2019; Emiliana, 2024b). Its commitment to innovation and quality has raised the global perception of Chilean wines, showing the country's potential as one of the central wine-producing regions. Family businesses have created jobs, supported local communities and contributed to the economic development of Chile's wine regions.

The global consumer was slowly becoming more aware of the products they were purchasing, not just for health reasons but also for their environmental and social impact.

> At Emiliana Vineyard, we not only believe that organic and biodynamic agriculture is the best way to create wines, but we are sure that it is a way of life that allows us to envision a future with respect and wisdom. We are organic by conviction, by ideology, and by love. (Emiliana, 2024a, para. 1–2)

These concrete actions demonstrate that this family business has a proactive sustainability strategy. Its motivations in making sustainability decisions go beyond legal compliance and rely on beliefs, values and a long-term vision, even sacrificing short-term financial profitability.

José Guilisasti,[1] one of the owners, stated:

> Life is full of opportunities, and Emiliana Vineyards is one of them, where, united by a common passion, we have managed to produce high-quality wines with their own identity, achieving the most authentic expression of the terroir through organic and biodynamic agriculture, respecting the true value of the company, which is caring for people and the environment. We do what we are. (CNN Chile, 2012)

Although most companies in the wine sector are family-owned (Delmas & Gergaud, 2014), Emiliana Vineyards exemplifies the family's influence materialised in a long-term vision, family reputation, nurturing shared values, a sense of belonging and going beyond regulation. These factors lead to implementing sustainable initiatives with beneficial effects on the community, people and the environment.

---

[1]José Guilisasti passed away in November 2014.

Viña Emiliana: Like a Dream

This innovative venture was born in the late 1990s when its founders, Rafael, and José Guilisasti, realised that the market was beginning to change.

Emiliana Vineyard is the largest organic winery globally, with more than 800 hectares (approximately 2,000 acres) of certified vineyards, and the first in Chile and seventh in the world to obtain ISO 14001 (Environmental Management) certification (Emiliana, 2024a). The company produced the first wine in Latin America to obtain biodynamic certification and certified social responsibility for its good working conditions and for being a fair and transparent organisation. Additionally, it has obtained biodynamic and carbon neutral certifications and a vegan certification (Vegan Society), which guarantees that it does not use animal by-products to make its organic and biodynamic wines. In 2012, Emiliana Vineyard was elected Green Winery of the Year by the English magazine Drinks Business.

This family-owned company is an example of sustainability to follow. It has correctly incorporated the Triple Bottom Line Model (Elkington, 1997) in processing raw materials from the vineyard and in the transformation and finished products. The company has also introduced multiple initiatives concerning quality of life and social responsibility to help the community. These initiatives include educational scholarships, integrating students and teachers into organic farming and nursery management and direct support to small entrepreneurial families within the community. Another initiative is creating a mobile library to bring reading closer to the community and expand the coverage of local libraries, among others.

The Guilisasti family, one of the most prominent families in the Chilean wine industry, has played a pivotal role in Emiliana's success. The family's vision and leadership have been instrumental in positioning Emiliana as a leader in sustainable winemaking. The Guilisasti family recognised from the beginning the importance of sustainability in viticulture. The vision devised by the family business has led to the transformation of Emiliana into an organic and biodynamic winery.

Like any family business, family involvement has been vital to implementing innovative practices that improve environmental sustainability and wine quality. Under the direction of the Guilisasti family, Emiliana has balanced its commitment to caring for the environment with the pursuit of excellence in winemaking. This dual approach has been key to the winery's reputation and success.

The success of Viña Emiliana has had a significant impact on the Chilean wine industry, setting a benchmark in sustainable practices. The winery's achievements have shown that it is possible to produce world-class wines while maintaining a deep respect for the environment. This has encouraged other producers to explore and adopt organic and sustainable viticulture methods, contributing to the overall improvement of environmental practices in the industry.

A Dream Alignment With SDG#15

As a dream of the family, they thought of creating the first sustainable, organic and biodynamic winery in South America. In particular, the plan considered a 10-year timeline that included:

- The first organic vineyard with sustainable ecosystem management (Cain, 2019): Organic vineyards represent an agricultural practice that closely aligns with SDG#15: Life on Land. Vineyards in general can protect and restore land ecosystems by adopting organic farming methods while promoting sustainable land use, this aligns with the goal of achieving SDG#15.1. Viña Emiliana has achieved this by implementing practices such as covering crops, minimum tillage and composting.
- In addition to the above, the Vineyard has efficiently used water by incorporating techniques such as drip irrigation and has even gone a step further by collecting rainwater (Emiliana, 2024b), a testament to the company's commitment to sustainability and alignment with SDG#15.1. The company has integrated pest management strategies as part of its plan, focusing on biological controls such as incorporating beneficial insects and pheromone traps.
- New composting techniques: This practice enriches the soil with organic matter and improves its structure and fertility (Emiliana, 2024b), which aims to assist in achieving SDG#15.3, restoring land and soil.
- Incorporating cover crops: Planting cover crops between rows of vines prevents soil erosion, improves organic matter and promotes biodiversity (Emiliana, 2024b), aligning with the aim of achieving SDG#15.4.
- Promote crop rotation and intercropping: These practices improve soil nutrient cycling and reduce the accumulation of pests and diseases (The Drink Business, 2024).
- Improvement of healthy soils resistant to erosion and drought. They support diverse microbial communities and are critical to the long-term sustainability of vineyards (The Drink Business, 2024).

SDG#15.5 aims to protect biodiversity and natural habitats through actions being taken to reduce the degradation of natural habitats and halt the loss of biodiversity (United Nations, n.d.). Viña Emiliana embraces this target through its organic vineyards by adopting above-standard biodiversity practices when compared to conventional vineyards. Practices supporting Viña Emiliana's biodiversity include habitat creation, reduced or minimal use of chemicals, and eliminating synthetic inputs such as pesticides and fertilizers.

Commitment to Organic and Biodynamic Practices

Viña Emiliana transitioned to organic farming in the late 1990s, driven by the vision to produce wines that are exceptional in quality and respectful of the environment and human health. The winery's dedication to sustainability is evident in several critical practices:

- Organic farming: Emiliana avoids pesticides, herbicides and synthetic fertilisers and turns to natural alternatives. This approach helps maintain soil health, improve biodiversity and reduce pollution (Emiliana, 2024b), which is in line with SDG#15.5.

- Biodynamic Viticulture: Following the principles of biodynamic agriculture, Emiliana incorporates holistic practices that consider the vineyard as a living ecosystem (Cain, 2019; Emiliana, 2024b). These include using biodynamic preparations, aligning agricultural practices with lunar and cosmic rhythms and maintaining biodiversity within the vineyard (Billabong Retreat, 2023). These practices help Emiliana in aligning itself with SDG#15.1 in terms of conserving and restoring terrestrial ecosystems.
- Renewable Energy and Water Conservation: The winery employs renewable energy sources and implements water conservation strategies to minimise its environmental footprint.

These practices contribute to the sustainability of the vineyard and enhance the quality and distinctiveness of Emiliana wines, which are characterised by their purity and expression of the terroir.[2]

Awards and Recognition of Its Commitment to Sustainability

Viña Emiliana's commitment to sustainability has earned it numerous recognitions and certifications, including:

- *Organic Certification*: Emiliana's vineyards are certified organic by various international organisations, ensuring compliance with rigorous standards such as Regenerative Organic Certification (ROC) and the certification for organic grape and production systems by IMO, Switzerland (Emiliana, 2024c; Noble Green Wines, 2024).
- *Biodynamic Certification*: The winery is also Demeter[3] certified for its biodynamic practices (Emiliana, 2024c).

Conclusion

The Guilisasti family's vision, leadership and commitment to sustainability have made them key figures in the Chilean wine industry. Their pioneering organic and biodynamic viticulture efforts through Viña Emiliana have set a benchmark for sustainable wine production. Along with Emiliana's innovation in sustainable initiatives, Viña Concha y Toro's leadership has helped establish Chile as a leading player in the global wine market. The legacy of the Guilisasti family continues to influence and inspire the Chilean wine industry, promoting a future where quality, innovation and sustainability go hand in hand.

---

[2]Terroir is a term used in the wine world to encompass the combination of factors that influence the characteristics of grapes grown in a specific region. It includes various environmental factors like climate, soil, topography and geography.

[3]DEMETER symbol indicates that produce has been grown and processed according to the standards of the Bio-Dynamic Research Institute.

References

Basso, F., Ibarra, G., Pezoa, R., & Varas, M. (2024). Horizontal collaboration in the wine supply chain planning: A Chilean case study. *Journal of the Operational Research Society*, *75*(1), 67–84.

Billabong Retreat. (2023). *Embracing biodiversity for a sustainable future.* Billabong Retreat. https://billabongretreat.com.au/2023/12/05/biodynamic-farming/

Cain, S. (2019, April 25). *Meet the unexpected: This winemaker is using biodynamics to elevate Chile's most popular grape.* VinePair. https://vinepair.com/articles/meet-the-unexpected-this-winemaker-is-using-biodynamics-to-elevate-chiles-most-popular-grape/

Cederberg, P., Gustafsson, J. G., & Mårtensson, A. (2008). Potential for organic Chilean wine. *Acta Agriculturae Scandinavica Section B, Soil and Plant Science*, *59*(1), 19–32. https://doi.org/10.1080/09064710701834713

Charlin, V., Cifuentes, A., Gonzales, L., & Larrain, F. (2023). Weather and wine quality in Chile's Casablanca Valley. *Journal of Wine Research*, *34*(2), 122–139.

CNN Chile (Producer). (2012). *La interesante apuesta por el vino orgánico y biodinámico* [Video]. YouTube. https://www.youtube.com/watch?v=bUkfRbpQQwQ

Concha y Toro. (2024a). *Our history.* Concha y Toro. https://conchaytoro.com/en/about-us/our-history/

Concha y Toro. (2024b). *Isabel Mitarakis.* Concha y Toro. https://conchaytoro.com/en/winemakers/isabel-mitarakis-guilisasti/

Delmas, M. A., & Gergaud, O. (2014). Sustainable certification for future generations: The case of family business. *Family Business Review*, *27*(3), 228–243.

Elkington, J. (1997). *Cannibals with forks: The triple bottom line of 21st century business.* Capstone.

Emiliana. (2024a). *Who we are: History.* Emiliana. https://www.emiliana.cl/en/nosotros/historia

Emiliana. (2024b). *Why organic wines.* Emiliana. https://www.emiliana.cl/en/agricultura-regenerativa/agricultura-organica/

Emiliana. (2024c). *Our commitment.* Emiliana. https://www.emiliana.cl/en/nuestro-compromiso/

Lluch, A. (2008, December 18). *Interview with Rafael Guilisasti Gana, interviewed by Andrea Lluch, Santiago.* Creating Emerging Markets Oral History Collection, Baker Library Historical Collections, Harvard Business School.

Muhie, S. H. (2023). Concepts, principles, and application of biodynamic farming: A review. *Circular Economy and Sustainability*, *3*(1), 291–304.

Müller, C., & Randolph, R. V. (2024). Sustainability in family and nonfamily businesses in the wine industry. *Journal of Evolutionary Studies in Business*, *9*(1), 152–177.

Noble Green Wines. (2024). Producer spotlight – Emilian Organic Vineyards. *Noble Green Wines.* https://noblegreenwines.co.uk/articles/category/guides/producer-spotlight-emiliana-organic-vineyards

Sachs, J., Schmidt-Traub, G., Kroll, C., Lafortune, G., Fuller, G., & Woelm, F. (2020). *The sustainable development goals and COVID-19. Sustainable development report, 2020.* Cambridge University Press.

The Drink Business. (2024). Sense and sustainability: How wine producers are protecting the environment. https://www.thedrinksbusiness.com/2019/01/sense-and-sustainability-how-wine-producers-are-protecting-the-environment/8/a

United Nations. (n.d.). *Goal 15 life on land*. United Nations. https://www.globalgoals.org/goals/15-life-on-land/

Vinos de Chile Annual Mémoire. (2023). *Vinos de Chile*. Vinos de Chile. https://www.winesofchile.org/sustainability/

Index

www.ingramcontent.com/pod-product-compliance
Lightning Source LLC
Chambersburg PA
CBHW061257220326
41599CB00028B/5679